Be Daring

New Testament BE Books by Warren Wiersbe

Be Loyal *(Matthew)*
Be Diligent *(Mark)*
Be Compassionate *(Luke 1–13)*
Be Courageous *(Luke 14–24)*
Be Alive *(John 1–12)*
Be Transformed *(John 13–21)*
Be Dynamic *(Acts 1–12)*
Be Daring *(Acts 13–28)*
Be Right *(Romans)*
Be Wise *(1 Corinthians)*
Be Encouraged *(2 Corinthians)*
Be Free *(Galatians)*
Be Rich *(Ephesians)*
Be Joyful *(Philippians)*
Be Complete *(Colossians)*
Be Ready *(1 & 2 Thessalonians)*
Be Faithful *(1 & 2 Timothy, Titus, Philemon)*
Be Confident *(Hebrews)*
Be Mature *(James)*
Be Hopeful *(1 Peter)*
Be Alert *(2 Peter, 2 & 3 John, Jude)*
Be Real *(1 John)*
Be Victorious *(Revelation)*

Be
Daring

Warren W.
Wiersbe

Chariot VICTOR
PUBLISHING
A DIVISION OF COOK COMMUNICATIONS

In this book, Scripture references without book designations (e.g., 3:2; 7:5; 20:6) always refer to the Book of Acts. All other references include the Bible book designations (e.g., Luke 3:5; 6:2; John 3:16), but where confusion may result, Book of Acts references also include the Acts designation. References without chapter designation (e.g., vv. 2, 6-10) relate to the Acts passage under consideration in the study.

9   10   Printing/Year   00   99   98   97

Recommended Dewey Decimal Classification: 228
Suggested Subject Headings: BIBLE, N.T.; BOOK OF ACTS

Library of Congress Catalog Card Number: 87-62471
ISBN: 0-89693-447-0
Victor Books is an imprint of ChariotVictor Publishing,
a division of Cook Communications, Colorado Springs, Colorado 80918
Cook Communications, Paris, Ontario
Kingsway Communications, Eastbourne, England

CONTENTS

Dedicated to

DICK and MARGE WINCHELL
and the missionary family of
The Evangelical Alliance Mission (TEAM)
serving Jesus Christ around the world

In March 1995 Warren Wiersbe became Writer in Residence
at Cornerstone College in Grand Rapids, Michigan,
and Distinguished Professor of Preaching at
Grand Rapids Baptist Seminary. He also serves as
senior contributing editor in the field of
pastoral ministry at Baker Book House.

PREFACE

The eminent American psychologist William James said, "It is only by risking our persons from one hour to another that we live at all." And the popular motivational expert Earl Nightingale claims, "Wherever there is danger, there lurks opportunity; wherever there is opportunity, there lurks danger."

Paul and his friends would say a hearty "Amen!" to these two statements and would back up their votes with the testimony of their lives. After all, in the early church, Paul and Barnabas were known as "men that have hazarded their lives for the name of our Lord Jesus Christ" (15:26).

For this reason, *Be Daring* seems to be the logical title for this study of Acts 13–28, a companion volume to *Be Dynamic*, which covers Acts 1–12. If we have the dynamic of the Holy Spirit in our lives, then surely we will not be satisfied with "Christian living as usual." We will want the Lord to put us where the real action is and make us daring pioneers instead of comfortable spectators.

"The fishermen know that the sea is dangerous and the storm terrible," wrote Vincent van Gogh, "but they have never found these dangers sufficient reason for remaining ashore." If danger does not stop the commercial fisherman, whose main concern is income, why should it stop those who are fishing for souls and have eternity's values in view?

Yes, the time has come for more of us to BE DARING!

WARREN W. WIERSBE

A Suggested Outline of the Book of Acts

Key theme: The expansion of the church in the world
Key verse: Acts 1:8

I. THE MINISTRY OF PETER (1–12)
Jerusalem the center
Ministry primarily to Israel
1. Peter and the Jews, 1–7
2. Peter and the Samaritans, 8
3. The conversion of Paul, 9
4. Peter and the Gentiles, 10–11
5. Peter's arrest and deliverance, 12

II. THE MINISTRY OF PAUL (13–28)
Syrian Antioch the center
Ministry primarily to the Gentiles
1. Paul's first missionary journey, 13–14
2. The Jerusalem conference, 15
3. Paul's second missionary journey, 16:1–18:22
4. Paul's third missionary journey, 18:23–21:17
5. Paul's arrest and voyage to Rome, 21:18–28:31

1

God Opens the Doors

Acts 13–14

We usually identify the preaching of the Gospel with the quiet rural villages of Palestine where the Lord Jesus ministered. For this reason, many Christians are surprised to learn that the church in the Book of Acts was almost entirely *urban*. Historian Wayne A. Meeks writes that "within a decade of the crucifixion of Jesus, the village culture of Palestine had been left behind, and the Greco-Roman city became the dominant environment of the Christian movement" (*The First Urban Christians*, page 11).

The church began in Jerusalem, and then spread to other cities, including Samaria, Damascus, Caesarea, and Antioch in Syria. At least forty different cities are named in Acts. From Antioch, Paul and his helpers carried the Gospel throughout the then known world. In fact, the record given in Acts 13–28 is almost a review of ancient geography. About the year 56, the Apostle Paul was able to write, "So that from Jerusalem, and round about unto Illyricum, I have fully preached the Gospel of Christ" (Rom. 15:19). What a record!

In these two chapters, Dr. Luke described Paul's ministry in six different cities, beginning and ending at Antioch.

1. Antioch in Syria—Decision (13:1-5)

That sainted missionary to India and Persia, Henry Martyn, once said, "The Spirit of Christ is the spirit of missions, and the nearer we get to Him, the more intensely missionary we must become." Paul (Saul) and Barnabas had that experience as they ministered in Antioch and were called by the Spirit to take the Gospel to the Roman world.

Until now, Jerusalem had been the center of ministry, and Peter had been the key apostle. But from this point on, Antioch in Syria would become the new center (11:19ff), and Paul the new leader. The Gospel was on the move!

Luke listed five different men who were ministering in the church: *Barnabas*, whom we have already met (Acts 4:36-37; 9:27; and 11:22-26); *Simeon*, who may have been from Africa since he was nicknamed "Black"; *Lucius*, who came from Cyrene and may have been one of the founders of the church in Antioch (11:20); *Manaen*, who was an intimate friend (or perhaps an adopted foster brother) of Herod Antipas, who had killed John the Baptist; and *Saul* (Paul), last on the list but soon to become first.

These men were serving as "prophets and teachers" in a local church. The prophets helped lay the foundation for the church as they proclaimed the Word of God (Eph. 2:20; 1 Cor. 14:29-32). They were more "forth-tellers" than "foretellers," although at times the prophets did announce things to come (11:27-30). The "teachers" helped to ground the converts in the doctrines of the faith (2 Tim. 2:2).

God had already called Paul to minister to the Gentiles (9:15; 21:17-21), and now He summoned Barnabas to labor with him. The church confirmed their calling, commissioned the men, and sent them forth. It is the ministry of the Holy Spirit, working through the local church, to equip and enlist believers to go forth and serve. The modern mission board is only a "sending agency" that expedites the work authorized by the local church.

Barnabas and Paul took John Mark with them as their assistant. He was a cousin to Barnabas (Col. 4:10), and his mother's home in Jerusalem was a gathering place for the believers (Acts 12:12). It is likely that it was Peter who led John Mark to faith in Christ (1 Peter 5:13). John Mark no doubt helped Barnabas and Paul in numerous ways, relieving them of tasks and details that would have interfered with their important ministry of the Word.

2. Paphos—Deception (13:6-12)

It was logical to go first to Cyprus, for this was the home of Barnabas (4:36). Luke gives us no details of the ministry in Salamis, the great commercial center at the east end of the island. We trust that some people did believe the Gospel and that a local assembly was formed. The men then moved ninety miles to Paphos on the west end of the island, and there they met their first opposition.

Paphos was the capital of Cyprus, and the chief Roman official there was Sergius Paulus, "an understanding man" who wanted to hear the Word of God. He was opposed by a Jewish false prophet named "Son of Jesus [Joshua]." It is unusual to find a *Jewish* false prophet and sorcerer, for the Jews traditionally shunned such demonic activities. The name *Elymas* means "sorcerer" or "wise man" (cf. the "wise men" of Matt. 2).

This event is an illustration of the lesson that Jesus taught in the Parable of the Tares (Matt. 13:24-30, 36-43): wherever the Lord sows His true children (the wheat), Satan comes along and sows a counterfeit (the tares), a child of the devil. Paul recognized that Elymas was a child of the devil (John 8:44), and he inflicted blindness upon the false prophet as a judgment from God. This miracle was also evidence to Sergius Paulus that Paul and Barnabas were servants of the true God and preached the true message of salvation (Heb. 2:4). The Roman official believed and was saved.

Verse 9 of Acts 13 is the first place you find the familiar name *Paul* in the New Testament. As a Jewish Roman citizen, the apostle's full name was probably "Saul Paulus," for many Jews had both Jewish and Roman names.

3. Perga—Desertion (13:13)

Why did John Mark desert his friends and return to Jerusalem? Perhaps he was just plain homesick, or he may have become unhappy because Paul had begun to take over the leadership from Mark's cousin Barnabas. (Note "Paul and his company" in v. 13.) Mark was a devoted Jew, and he may have felt uncomfortable with the saved Gentiles. Some students think that John Mark's return to Jerusalem helped start the opposition of the legalistic Judaizers who later opposed Paul (see Acts 15 and the Epistle to the Galatians).

Another possibility is the fear of danger as the party moved into new and difficult areas. But whatever the cause of his defection, John Mark did something so serious that Paul did not want him back on his "team" again! (15:36ff) Later, Paul would enlist Timothy to take John Mark's place (16:1-5). John Mark did redeem himself and was eventually accepted and approved by Paul (2 Tim. 4:11).

During my years of ministry as a pastor and as a member of several mission boards, I have seen first-term workers do what John Mark did; and it has always been heartbreaking. But I have also seen some of them restored to missionary service, thanks to the prayers and encouragement of God's people. A.T. Robertson said that Mark "flickered in the crisis," but the light did not completely go out. This is an encouragement to all of us.

4. Antioch in Pisidia—Disputation (13:14-52)

Paul and Barnabas traveled 100 miles north and about 3,600 feet up to get to this important city on the Roman road. As you follow Paul's journeys in Acts, you will notice that he selected strategic cities, planted churches in them, and went on from the churches to evangelize the surrounding areas. You will also notice that, where it was possible, he started his ministry in the local synagogue, for he had a great burden for his people (Rom. 9:1-5; 10:1), and he found in the synagogue both Jews and Gentiles ready to hear the Word of God.

This is the first of Paul's sermons recorded in the Book of Acts, and it may be divided into three parts, each of which is introduced by the phrase "men and brethren."

Part 1—Preparation (16-25). In this section, Paul reviewed the history of Israel, climaxing with the ministry of John the Baptist and the coming of their Messiah. He made it clear that it was God who was at work in and for Israel, preparing the way for the coming of the promised Messiah. He also reminded his hearers that the nation had not always been faithful to the Lord and the covenant, but had often rebelled. Every pious Jew knew that the Messiah would come from David's family, and that a prophet would announce His coming beforehand. John the Baptist was that prophet.

Part 2—Declaration (26-37). As Paul addressed both the Jews and the Gentile "God-fearers" in the congregation, he changed his approach from third person ("they") to second person ("you"). He explained to them why their leaders in Jerusalem rejected and crucified the nation's Messiah. It was not because they had not read or heard the message of the prophets, but because they did not understand the message. Furthermore, the crucifixion of Jesus of Nazareth was even promised in the prophets. (Peter took this same approach in his second message, 3:12-18.)

It was the resurrection of Jesus Christ that was the crucial event: "But God raised Him from the dead" (v. 30). (See verses 33-34 and 37, and note that "raised" in verses 22-23 means "brought.") Paul has declared the Gospel to them, "the word of this salvation" (v. 26) and "the glad tidings" (v. 32). Christ died, He was buried, and He arose again!

Since Paul was addressing a synagogue congregation, he used the Old Testament Scriptures to support his argument. In verse 33, Psalm 2:7 is quoted; and note that it refers to the *resurrection* of Christ, not to the birth of Christ. The "virgin tomb" (John 19:41) was like a "womb" that gave birth to Jesus Christ in resurrection glory.

Then he quoted Isaiah 55:3, referring to the covenant that God made with David, "the sure mercies of David." God had promised David that from him the Messiah would come (2 Sam. 7:12-17). This was an "everlasting covenant" with a throne to be established forever (2 Sam. 7:13, 16). If Jesus is the Messiah, and He died and remained dead, this covenant could never be fulfilled. Therefore, Jesus had to be raised from the dead or the covenant would prove false.

His third quotation was from Psalm 16:10, the same passage Peter quoted in his message at Pentecost (2:24-28). The Jews considered Psalm 16 to be a messianic psalm, and it was clear that this promise did not apply to David, who was dead, buried, and decayed. It had to apply to Jesus Christ, the Messiah.

Part 3—Application (38-41). Paul had declared the good news to them (v. 32), and now all that remained was to make the personal application and "draw the net." He told them that through faith in Jesus Christ, they could have two blessings that the Law could never provide: the forgiveness of their sins and justification before the throne of God.

Justification is the act of God whereby He declares the believing sinner righteous in Jesus Christ. It has to do with the believer's standing before the throne of God. The Jews were taught that God justified the righteous and punished the wicked (2 Chron. 6:22-23). But God justifies the ungodly who will put their faith in Jesus Christ (Rom. 4:1-8).

The Law cannot justify the sinner; it can only condemn him (Gal. 2:16; Rom. 3:19-20). God not only forgives our sins, but He also gives us the very righteousness of Christ and puts it on our account! This was certainly good news delivered by Paul to that searching congregation of Jews and Gentiles who had no peace in their hearts, even though they were religious.

Paul closed his message with a note of warning taken from Habakkuk 1:5 (and see Isa. 29:14). In Habakkuk's day, the "unbelievable work" God was doing was the raising up of the Chaldeans to chasten His people, a work so remarkable that nobody would believe it. After all, why would God use an evil pagan nation to punish His own chosen people, sinful though they might be? God was using Gentiles to punish Jews! But the "wonderful work" in Paul's day was that God was using the Jews to save the Gentiles!

What was the result? Many Jews and Gentile proselytes believed and associated with Paul and Barnabas. The Gentiles were especially excited about Paul's message and wanted him to tell them more, which he did the next Sabbath. The people had done a good job of spreading the news, because a great crowd gathered. They were probably predominantly Gentiles, which made the Jews envious and angry.

Paul's final message in the synagogue declared that God had sent the Word to the Jews first (Acts 3:26; Rom. 1:16), but they had now rejected it. Therefore, Paul would now take the Good News to the Gentiles; and he quoted Isaiah 49:6 to back up his decision. (Note also Luke 2:29-32.) He was ready to go to the ends of the earth to win souls to Christ!

Acts 13:48 gives us the divine side of evangelism, for God has His elect people (Eph. 1:4). The word translated *ordained* means "enrolled," and indicates that God's people have their names written in God's book (Luke 10:20; Phil. 4:3). But verse 49 is the human side of evangelism: if we do not preach the Word, then nobody can believe and be saved. It takes both. (See 2 Thes. 2:13-14 and Rom. 10:13-15.)

The unbelieving Jews were not going to sit back and let Paul and Barnabas take over. First, they disputed with them, and then brought legal action against them and expelled them from their borders. The missionaries were not discouraged: they shook off the dust of their feet against them (Luke 9:5 and 10:11) and went to the next town, leaving behind them a group of joyful disciples.

5. Iconium—Division (14:1-7)

This city, more Greek than Roman, was in the Roman province of Galatia. Paul's ministry in the synagogue was singularly blessed and a multitude of Jews and Gentiles believed. Once again, the unbelieving Jews stirred up hatred and opposition, but the missionaries stayed on and witnessed boldly for Christ. (Note the "therefore" in v. 3.)

God also enabled the men to perform signs and wonders as their "credentials" that they were indeed the servants of the true God. (See 15:12; Heb. 2:4; Gal. 3:5.) Faith is not based on miracles (Luke 16:27-31; John 2:23-25), but faith can be bolstered by miracles. The important thing is "the word of His grace" that performs the work of His grace (14:26).

The result? The city was divided and the Christians were threatened with public disgrace and stoning. Obedient to their Lord's counsel in Matthew 10:23, they fled from that area into a different Roman district and continued to minister the Word of God.

6. Lystra—Delusion (14:8-20)

Lystra was in the Roman province of Galatia, about eighteen miles southwest of Iconium. This was the first of three visits

Paul made to this city, and an eventful visit it was! On his second missionary journey, Paul enlisted Timothy in Lystra (16:1-5); and he made a visit to this church on his third journey as well (18:23). We should note four different responses during this visit.

The crippled man's response to the Word (8-10). Both Peter and Paul healed men who were lame from birth (Acts 3). Had their lameness been caused by disease or accident, the cure might have been attributed to a sudden change in their health. As it was, the cure was obviously miraculous.

The word translated "speak" in verse 9 means ordinary conversation, although it can refer to formal speaking. It is likely that Paul was simply conversing with some of the citizens in the marketplace, telling them about Jesus, and the lame man overheard what he said. The Word produced faith (Rom. 10:17) and faith brought healing.

The crowd's response to the crippled man (11-13). Miracles by themselves do not produce either conviction or faith. They must be accompanied by the Word (14:3). This was a superstitious crowd that interpreted events in the light of their own mythology. They identified Barnabas as Jupiter (Zeus), the chief of the gods; and Paul, the speaker, they identified with Mercury (Hermes), the messenger of the gods. Jupiter was the patron deity of the city, so this was a great opportunity for the priest of Jupiter to become very important and lead the people in honoring their god.

The apostles' response to the crowd (14-19). How easy it would have been to accept this worship and try to use the honor as a basis for teaching the people the truth, but that is not the way God's true servants minister (2 Cor. 4:1-2; 1 Thes. 2:1-5). Paul and Barnabas opposed what they were doing and boldly told the people that the gods of Lystra were "vanities."

Paul's message was not based on the Old Testament, because this was a pagan Gentile audience. He started with the witness of God in Creation (see 17:22ff). He made it clear that there is but one God who is the living God, the giving God, and the forgiving God. And He has been patient with the sinning nations (17:30) and has not judged them for their sins as they deserve.

The crowd quieted down, but when some troublemaking Jews arrived from Antioch and Iconium, the crowd followed their lead and stoned Paul. One minute, Paul was a god to be worshiped; the next minute, he was a criminal to be slain! Emerson called a mob "a society of bodies voluntarily bereaving themselves of reason." Often this is true.

The disciples' response to Paul (v. 20). There were new believers in Lystra, and this was a crisis situation for them. They were a minority, their leader had been stoned, and their future looked very bleak. But they stood by Paul! It is likely that they joined hearts and prayed for him, and this is one reason God raised him up. Was Paul dead? We are not told. This is the only stoning he ever experienced (2 Cor. 11:25), but from it came glory to God. It may have been this event that especially touched Timothy and eventually led to his association with Paul (2 Tim. 3:10).

7. Antioch in Syria—Declaration (14:21-28)

On their return trip to Antioch, the missionaries were engaged in several important ministries.

First, they preached the Gospel and made disciples ("taught many"). It is difficult to understand how they got back into the cities from which they had been expelled, but the Lord opened the doors.

Second, they strengthened ("confirmed") the believers in the things of Christ and encouraged ("exhorted") them to continue in the faith. Continuance is a proof of true faith in Jesus Christ (John 8:31-32; Acts 2:42). Paul made it very clear that living the Christian life was not an easy thing and that they would all have to expect trials and sufferings before they would see the Lord in glory.

Third, they organized the churches (vv. 23-25). The local church is both an organism and an organization, for if an organism is not organized, it will die! Paul and Barnabas ordained spiritual leaders and gave them the responsibility of caring for the flock. If you compare Titus 1:5 and 7, you will see that "elder" and "bishop" (overseer) refer to the same office, and both are equivalent to "pastor" (shepherd).

The word translated *ordained* means "to elect by a show of hands." It is possible that Paul chose the men and the congregation voted its approval, or that the people selected them by vote and Paul ordained them (see 6:1-6).

Finally, they reported to their "sending church" on the work God had done (vv. 26-28). They had been gone at least a year, and it must have been exciting for them and for the church when they arrived back home. They had, by the grace of God, fulfilled the work God had given them to do; and they joyfully reported the blessings to the church family.

This is perhaps the first "missionary conference" in church history, and what a conference it must have been! A church officer once said to me, "I don't care how much money you want for missions, I'll give it; but *just don't make me listen to missionaries speak!*" I felt sorry for him that his spiritual temperature was so low that he could not listen to reports of what God was doing in the difficult corners of the harvest field.

As you review Paul's first missionary journey, you can see the principles by which he operated, principles that are still applicable today.

He worked primarily in the key cities and challenged the believers to take the message out to the more remote areas. The Gospel works in the population centers, and we must carry it there.

He used one approach with the synagogue congregations and another with the Gentiles. He referred the Jews and Jewish proselytes to the Old Testament Scriptures; but when preaching to the Gentiles, he emphasized the God of creation and His goodness to the nations. His starting point was different, but his finishing point was the same: faith in the Lord Jesus Christ.

He majored on establishing and organizing local churches. Jesus had the local church in mind when He gave what we call "The Great Commission" (Matt. 28:19-20). After we make disciples ("teach"), we must baptize them (the responsibility primarily of a local church) and then teach them the Word of God. Merely winning people to Christ is but fulfilling one-third of the Commission! It takes the local assembly of believers to help us fulfill all of what Jesus commanded us to do.

He grounded the believers in the Word of God. This is the only source of strength and stability when persecution comes, as it inevitably does come. Paul did not preach a popular "success Gospel" that painted a picture of an easy Christian life.

The amazing thing is that Paul and his associates did all of this without the modern means of transportation and communication that we possess today. Dr. Bob Pierce used to say to us in Youth For Christ, "Others have done so much with so little, while we have done so little with so much!" The wasted wealth of American believers alone, if invested in world evangelization, might lead to the salvation of millions of lost people.

Paul and Barnabas announced that the "door of faith" had been opened to the Gentiles.

That door is still open, to Jews and Gentiles alike—to a whole world! Walk through that open door and help take the Gospel to others.

Be daring!

2
Don't Close the Doors!

Acts 15:1-35

The progress of the Gospel has often been hindered by people with closed minds who stand in front of open doors and block the way for others.

In 1786, when William Carey laid the burden of world missions before a ministerial meeting in Northampton, England, the eminent Dr. Ryland said to him, "Young man, sit down! When God pleases to convert the heathen, He will do it without your aid or mine!" More than one Spirit-filled servant of God has had to enter open doors of opportunity without the support of churches and religious leaders.

Paul and his associates faced this same challenge at the Jerusalem conference about twenty years after Pentecost. Courageously, they defended both the truth of the Gospel and the missionary outreach of the church. There were three stages in this event.

1. The Dispute (15:1-5)

It all started when some legalistic Jewish teachers came to Antioch and taught that the Gentiles, in order to be saved, had to be circumcised and obey the Law of Moses. These men were associated with the Jerusalem congregation but not authorized by it (15:24). Identified with the Pharisees (15:5), these teachers were "false brethren" who wanted to rob both Jewish and Gentile believers of their liberty in Christ (Gal. 2:1-10; 5:1ff).

It is not surprising that there were people in the Jerusalem church who were strong advocates of the Law of Moses but ignorant of the relationship between Law and grace. These people were Jews who had been trained to respect and obey the Law of Moses; and, after all, Romans, Galatians, and Hebrews had not yet been written! There was a large group of priests in the Jerusalem assembly (6:7), as well as people who still followed some of the Old Testament practices (see 21:20-26). It was a time of transition, and such times are always difficult.

What were these legalists actually doing and why were they so dangerous? They were attempting to mix Law and grace and to pour the new wine into the ancient brittle wineskins (Luke 5:36-39). They were stitching up the rent veil (Luke 23:45) and blocking the new and living way to God that Jesus had opened when He died on the cross (Heb. 10:19-25). They were rebuilding the wall between Jews and Gentiles that Jesus had torn down on the cross (Eph. 2:14-16). They were putting the heavy Jewish yoke on Gentile shoulders (Gal. 5:1; Acts 15:10) and asking the church to move out of the sunlight into the shadows (Heb. 10:1; Col. 2:16-17). They were saying, "A Gentile must first become a Jew before he can become a Christian! It is not sufficient for them simply to trust Jesus Christ. They must also obey Moses!"

Several important issues are involved here, not the least of which is the work of Christ on the cross as declared in the message of the Gospel (1 Cor. 15:1-8; Heb. 10:1-18). God pronounces a solemn anathema on anyone who preaches any other Gospel than the Gospel of the grace of God found in Jesus Christ His Son (Gal. 1:1-9). When any religious leader says, "Unless you belong to our group, you cannot be saved!" or "Unless you participate in our ceremonies and keep our rules, you cannot be saved!" he is adding to the Gospel and denying the finished work of Jesus Christ. Paul wrote his Epistle to the Galatians to make it clear that salvation is wholly by God's grace, through faith in Christ, *plus nothing!*

Another issue involved was the nature of the church's missionary program. If these legalists (we call them "the Judaizers") were correct, then Paul and Barnabas had been all wrong in their ministry. Along with preaching the Gospel, they should have been teaching the Gentiles how to live as good Jews. No wonder Paul and Barnabas debated and disputed with these false teachers! (15:2, 7) The Antioch believers were being "troubled" and "subverted" (v. 24), and this same confusion and disruption would soon spread to the Gentile churches Paul and Barnabas had founded. This was a declaration of war that Paul and Barnabas could not ignore.

God gave Paul a revelation instructing him to take the whole matter to the Jerusalem church leaders (Gal. 2:2), and to this the Antioch assembly agreed ("they" in 15:2). The gathering was not a "church council" in the denominational sense, but rather a meeting of the leaders who heard the various groups and then made their decision. Though the "mother church" in Jerusalem did have great influence, each local church was autonomous.

2. The Defense (15:6-18)
It appears that at least four different meetings were involved in this strategic conference: (1) a public welcome to Paul and his associates, 15:4; (2) a private meeting of Paul and the key leaders, Galatians 2:2; (3) a second public meeting at which the Judaizers presented their case, 15:5-6 and Galatians 2:3-5;

and (4) the public discussion described in Acts 15:6ff. In this public discussion, four key leaders presented the case for keeping the doors of grace open to the lost Gentiles.

Peter reviewed the past (vv. 6-11). We get the impression that Peter sat patiently while the disputing ("questioning") was going on, waiting for the Spirit to direct him. "He who answers a matter before he hears it, it is folly and shame to him" (Prov. 18:13, NKJV). Peter reminded the church of four important ministries that God had performed for the Gentiles, ministries in which he had played an important part.

First, God made a choice that Peter should preach the Gospel to the Gentiles (v. 7). Jesus had given the keys of the kingdom to Peter (Matt. 16:19), and he had used them to open the door of faith to the Jews (Acts 2), the Samaritans (Acts 8:14-17), and the Gentiles (Acts 10). The apostles and brethren in Judea had censured Peter for visiting the Gentiles and eating with them, but he had satisfactorily defended himself (11:1-18). Note that Peter made it clear that Cornelius and his household were saved by hearing and believing, not by obeying the Law of Moses.

Second, God gave the Holy Spirit to the Gentiles to bear witness that they truly were born again (v. 8). Only God can see the human heart; so, if these people had not been saved, God would never have given them the Spirit (Rom. 8:9). But they did not receive the Spirit by keeping the Law, but by believing God's Word (Acts 10:43-46; and see Gal. 3:2). Peter's message was "whoever believes in Him will receive remission of sins" (Acts 10:43, NKJV), not "whoever believes and obeys the Law of Moses."

Third, God erased a difference (vv. 9, 11). For centuries, God had put a difference between Jews and Gentiles, and it was the task of the Jewish religious leaders to protect and maintain that difference (Lev. 10:10; Ezek. 22:26; 44:23). Jesus taught that the Jewish dietary laws had nothing to do with inner holiness (Mark 7:1-23), and Peter had learned that lesson again when he had that vision on the housetop in Joppa (Acts 10:1ff).

Ever since the work of Christ on Calvary, God has made no difference between Jews and Gentiles as far as sin (Rom. 3:9, 22) or salvation (Rom. 10:9-13) are concerned. Sinners can have their hearts purified only by faith in Christ; salvation is not by keeping the Law (Acts 15:9). We would expect Peter to conclude his defense by saying, "They [the Gentiles] shall be saved even as we Jews," but he said just the reverse! "We [Jews] shall be saved, even as they!"

God's fourth ministry—and this was Peter's strongest statement—was the removing of the yoke of the Law (v. 10). The Law was indeed a yoke that burdened the Jewish nation, but that yoke has been taken away by Jesus Christ (see Gal. 5:1ff; Col. 2:14-17; Matt. 11:28-30). After all, the Law was given to the Jewish nation to protect them from the evils of the Gentile world and prepare them to bring the Messiah into the world (Gal. 4:1-7). The Law cannot purify the sinner's heart (Gal. 2:21), impart the gift of the Holy Spirit (Gal. 3:2), or give eternal life (Gal. 3:21). What the Law could not do, God did through His own Son (Rom. 8:1-4). Those who have trusted Christ have the righteousness of God's Law in their hearts and, through the Spirit, obey His will. They are not motivated by fear, but by love, for "love is the fulfilling of the Law" (Rom. 13:8-10).

Paul and Barnabas reported on the present (v. 12). Peter's witness made a great impact on the congregation because they sat in silence after he was finished. Then Paul and Barnabas stood up and told the group what God had done among the Gentiles through their witness. Dr. Luke devoted only one summary sentence to their report since he had already given it in detail in Acts 13 and 14. Paul and Barnabas were greatly respected by the church (see vv. 25-26) and their testimony carried a great deal of weight.

Their emphasis was on the miracles that God had enabled them to perform among the Gentiles. These miracles were proof that God was working with them (Mark 16:20; Acts 15:4) and that they were God's chosen messengers (Rom. 15:18-19; Heb. 2:2-4). "Does God give you His Spirit and work miracles among you because you observe the Law, or because you believe what you heard?" (Gal. 3:5, NIV) They had preached grace, not Law; and God had honored this message.

If you will review the record of the first missionary journey (Acts 13–14), you will see that the emphasis is on what God did in response to men's faith. See 13:8, 12, 39, 41, 48; 14:1, 22, 23, 27. Note also the emphasis on grace (13:43; 14:3, 26). God opened for the Gentiles "the door of faith," not "the door of Law." For that matter the Antioch church, which commissioned Paul and Barnabas, was founded by people who "believed and turned unto the Lord" (11:21) and experienced the grace of God (11:23). They were saved the same way sinners are saved today, "by grace, through faith" (Eph. 2:8-9).

Both Peter and Paul received from God special visions directing them to go to the Gentiles (10:1ff; 22:21). However, it was Paul whom God set apart as the apostle to the Gentiles (Eph. 3:1-12; Rom. 11:13; Gal. 2:6-10). If Gentile sinners had to obey the Law of Moses in order to be saved, then why did God give Paul the Gospel of grace and send him off to the Gentiles? God could just as well have sent Peter!

Peter reviewed God's ministries to the Gentiles in the past, and Paul and Barnabas reported on God's work among the Gentiles in that present day. James was the final speaker and he focused on the future.

James related it all to the future (vv. 13-18). James was a brother to Jesus (Gal. 1:19; Matt. 13:55) and the writer of the Epistle of James. He and his brethren were not believers in Christ until after the Resurrection (John 7:5; 1 Cor. 15:7; Acts

1:14). James had strong leanings toward the Law (there are at least ten references to law in his epistle), so he was most acceptable to the legalistic party in the Jerusalem church.

The key idea in James' speech is *agreement*. First, he expressed his full agreement with Peter that God was saving the Gentiles by grace. It must have startled the Judaizers when James called these saved Gentiles "a people for His [God's] name," because for centuries the Jews had carried that honorable title. (See Deut. 7:6; 14:2; 28:10.) Today, God is graciously calling out a people, the church, from both Jews and Gentiles. In fact, the Greek word for "church" (ekklesia) means "a called out assembly" (kaleo = to call; ek = out). But if they are called out, then their salvation is all of grace and not through the keeping of the Law!

The Judaizers did not understand how the Gentiles and the Jews related to each other in the church, or how the church fit into God's promise to establish a kingdom for Israel. The Old Testament declared both the salvation of the Gentiles (Isa. 2:2; 11:10) and the future establishing of a glorious kingdom for Israel (Isa. 11–12; 35; 60), but it did not explain how they related to each other. The legalists in the church were jealous for both the future glory of Israel and the past glory of Moses and the Law. It seemed to them that their acceptance of the Gentiles as "spiritual equals" jeopardized the future of Israel.

We today have a better grasp of this truth because Paul explained it in Ephesians 2 and 3 and Romans 9–11. Saved Jews and Gentiles are both members of the same body and "one in Christ Jesus" (Gal. 3:28). The truth about the church, the body of Christ, was a "mystery" (a sacred secret) hidden in past ages and revealed to the church by the Spirit. God's "mystery program" for the church does not cancel His great "prophecy program" for Israel. Paul makes it clear in Romans 9–11 that there is a future for Israel and that God will keep His "kingdom promises" to His people.

James also stated that the prophets also agreed with this conclusion, and he cited Amos 9:11-12 to prove his point. Note that he did not state that what Peter, Paul, and Barnabas had said was a *fulfillment* of this prophecy. He said that what Amos wrote *agreed with their testimony*. A careful reading of Amos 9:8-15 reveals that the prophet is describing events in the end times, when God will regather His people Israel to their land and bless them abundantly. If we "spiritualize" these promises, we rob them of their plain meaning and James' argument falls apart.

Amos also prophesied that the fallen house ("tent") of David would be raised up and God would fulfill His covenant with David that a king would sit on his throne (see 2 Sam. 7:25-29). This future king, of course, will be Jesus Christ, the Son of David (Luke 1:32; 2 Sam. 7:13, 16; Isa. 9:6-7) who will reign over Israel during the kingdom. In fact, the only Jew alive today who can prove his genealogy and defend his kingship is Jesus Christ!

God revealed these truths gradually to His people, but His plan had been settled from the beginning. Neither the cross nor the church were afterthoughts with God (Acts 2:23; 4:27-28; Eph. 1:4). The Judaizers thought that Israel had to "rise" in her glorious kingdom before the Gentiles could be saved, but God revealed that it was through Israel's "fall" that the Gentiles would find salvation (Rom. 11:11-16). At the time of the Jerusalem conference, David's house and throne indeed were fallen; but they would be restored one day and the kingdom established.

3. The Decision (15:19-35)

The leaders and the whole church (v. 22), directed by the Holy Spirit (v. 28), made a two-fold decision; a doctrinal decision about salvation, and a practical decision about how to live the Christian life.

The doctrinal decision we have already examined. The church concluded that Jews and Gentiles are all sinners before God and can be saved only by faith in Jesus Christ. There is one need, and there is but one Gospel to meet that need (Gal. 1:6-12). God has today but one program: He is calling out a people for His name. Israel is set aside but not cast away (Rom. 11:1ff); and when God's program for the church is completed, He will begin to fulfill His kingdom promises to the Jews.

But all doctrine must lead to duty. James emphasized this in his epistle (2:14-26), and so did Paul in his letters. It is not enough for us simply to accept a biblical truth; we must apply it personally in everyday life. Church problems are not solved by passing resolutions, but by practicing the revelations God gives us from His Word.

James advised the church to write to the Gentile believers and share the decisions of the conference. This letter asked for obedience to two *commands* and a willingness to agree to two personal *concessions*. The two commands were that the believers avoid idolatry and immorality, sins that were especially prevalent among the Gentiles (see 1 Cor. 8–10). The two concessions were that they willingly abstain from eating blood and meat from animals that had died by strangulation. The two commands do not create any special problems, for idolatry and immorality have always been wrong in God's sight, both for Jews and Gentiles. But what about the two concessions concerning food?

Keep in mind that the early church did a great deal of eating together and practicing of hospitality. Most churches met in homes, and some assemblies held a "love feast" in conjunction with the Lord's Supper (1 Cor. 11:17-34). It was probably not much different from our own potluck dinners. If the Gentile believers ate food that the Jewish believers considered "unclean," this would cause division in the church. Paul dealt clearly with this whole problem in Romans 14–15.

The prohibition against eating blood was actually given by God before the time of the Law (Gen. 9:4), and it was repeated by Moses (Lev. 17:11-14; Deut. 12:23). If an animal is killed by strangulation, some of the blood will remain in the body and make the meat unfit for Jews to eat. Hence, the admonition against strangulation. "Kosher" meat is meat that comes from clean animals that have been killed properly so that the blood has been totally drained from the body.

It is beautiful to see that this letter expressed the loving unity of people who had once been debating with each other and defending opposing views. The legalistic Jews willingly gave up insisting that the Gentiles had to be circumcised to be saved, and the Gentiles willingly accepted a change in their eating habits. It was a loving compromise that did not in any way affect the truth of the Gospel. As every married person and parent knows, there are times in a home when compromise is wrong, but there are also times when compromise is right. Wise Samuel Johnson said, "Life cannot subsist in society but by reciprocal concessions." The person who is always right, and who insists on having his or her own way, is difficult to live with happily.

What did this decision accomplish in a practical way? At least three things. First, it strengthened the unity of the church and kept it from splitting into two extreme "Law" and "grace" groups. President Eisenhower called the right kind of compromise "all of the usable surface. The extremes, right or left, are in the gutters." Again, this is not *doctrinal* compromise, for that is always wrong (Jude 3). Rather, it is learning to give and take in the practical arrangements of life so that people can live and work together in love and harmony.

Second, this decision made it possible for the church to present a united witness to the lost Jews (v. 21). For the most part, the church was still identified with the Jewish synagogue; and it is likely that in some cities, entire synagogue congregations believed on Jesus Christ—Jews, Gentile proselytes, and Gentile "God-fearers" together. If the Gentile believers abused their freedom in Christ and ate meat containing blood, this would offend both the saved Jews and their unsaved friends whom they were trying to win to Christ. It was simply a matter of not being a stumbling block to the weak or to the lost (Rom. 14:13-21).

Third, this decision brought blessing as the letter was shared with the various Gentile congregations. Paul and Barnabas, along with Judas and Silas, took the good news to Antioch; and the church rejoiced and was encouraged because they did not have to carry the burdensome yoke of the Law (vv. 30-31). On his second missionary journey, Paul shared the letter with the churches he had founded on his first missionary journey. The result was a strengthening of the churches' faith and an increase of their number (16:5).

We today can learn a great deal from this difficult experience of the early church. To begin with, problems and differences are opportunities for growth just as much as temptations for dissension and division. Churches need to work together and take time to listen, love, and learn. How many hurtful fights and splits could have been avoided if only some of God's people had given the Spirit time to speak and to work.

Most divisions are caused by "followers" and "leaders." A powerful leader gets a following, refuses to give in on even the smallest matter, and before long there is a split. Most church problems are not caused by doctrinal differences but by different viewpoints on practical matters. What color shall we paint the church kitchen? Can we change the order of the service? I heard of one church that almost split over whether the organ or the piano should be on the right side of the platform!

Christians need to learn the art of loving compromise. They need to have their priorities in order so they know when to fight for what is really important in the church. It is sinful to follow some impressive member of the church who is fighting to get his or her way on some minor issue that is not worth fighting about. Every congregation needs a regular dose of the love described in 1 Corinthians 13 to prevent division and dissension.

As we deal with our differences, we must ask, "How will our decisions affect the united witness of the church to the lost?" Jesus prayed that His people might be united so that the world might believe on Him (John 17:20-21). Unity is not uniformity, for unity is based on love and not law. There is a great need in the church for diversity in unity (Eph. 4:1-17), for that is the only way the body can mature and do its work in the world.

God has opened a wonderful door of opportunity for us to take the Gospel of God's grace to a condemned world. But there are forces in the church even today that want to close that door. There are people who are preaching "another gospel" that is not the Gospel of Jesus Christ.

Help keep that door open—and reach as many as you can!
Be daring!

3

More Open Doors

Acts 15:36–16:40

For the Apostle Paul, the church at Antioch was not a parking lot: it was a launching pad. He could never settle down to a "comfortable ministry" anywhere as long as there were open doors for the preaching of the Gospel.

Paul would have agreed enthusiastically with the words of Robertson McQuilken from his book *The Great Omission*: "In a world in which nine out of every ten people are lost, three out of four have never heard the way out, and one of every two cannot hear, the church sleeps on. Could it be we think there must be some other way? Or perhaps we don't really care that much." Paul cared—and so should we.

There were several new elements in this second journey that indicated that God was still at work, in spite of the seeming obstacles and personal difficulties that arose.

1. A New Partner (15:36-41)
Paul and Barnabas agreed on the importance of the trip, but they could not agree on the composition of the "team." Here were two dedicated men who had just helped bring unity to

the church, and yet they could not settle their own disagree-
ments! Disturbing and painful as these conflicts are, they are
often found in church history; and yet God is able to overrule
them and accomplish His purposes.

That Barnabas would champion John Mark is certainly no
surprise. He and Mark were cousins (Col. 4:10, NASB), and
the family ties would be strong. But even more, Barnabas was
the kind of man who eagerly tried to help others, which is
why the early church named him "son of encouragement"
(4:36). He was ready to give John Mark an opportunity to
serve the Lord and to prove himself. Barnabas "kept on insisting" (Wuest, *Expanded Translation*) that they take Mark
along.

But Paul was just as adamant that they *not* take Mark!
After all, on the first missionary journey, John Mark had de-
serted them to return home (13:13); and this was a mark of
weakness. The ministry was too important, and the work too
demanding, to enlist someone who might prove unreliable.

As the discussion continued, it turned into a real argument
(the word *paroxysm* comes from the word translated "contention"); and it seemed like the only solution was for the
friends to divide the territory and separate. Barnabas took
Mark and went to his native Cyprus, and Paul took Silas and
headed for Syria and Celicia (note v. 23).

Who was right? It really doesn't make much difference.
Perhaps both men were right on some things and wrong on
other things. We know that John Mark ultimately did succeed
in the ministry and that Paul came to love and appreciate
him. (See Phile. 23-24, Col. 4:10, and 2 Tim. 4:11.) Good and
godly people in the church do disagree; this is one of the
painful facts of life that we must accept. Paul looked at people
and asked, "What can they do for God's work?" while Barnabas looked at people and asked, "What can God's work do for
them?" Both questions are important to the Lord's work, and

sometimes it is difficult to keep things balanced.

Paul selected a new partner, Silas, a chief man in the church, a prophet (vv. 22, 32), and one chosen to take the Jerusalem conference decrees to the churches (v. 27). "Silas" is probably a Greek version of the name *Saul*. He was coauthor with Paul of the Thessalonian epistles, and he was the secretary for Peter's first epistle (5:12). Like Paul, he was a Roman citizen (Acts 16:37).

God changes His workmen, but His work goes right on. Now there were *two* missionary teams instead of one! If God had to depend on perfect people to accomplish His work, He would never ever get anything done. Our limitations and imperfections are good reasons for us to depend on the grace of God, for our sufficiency is from Him alone (2 Cor. 3:5).

2. A New Helper (16:1-5)

Paul and Silas approached their destination from the east, so they came first to Derbe and then to Lystra, just the reverse of the first journey (14:6-20). The preachers went from church to church, delivering the decrees and helping establish the believers in the faith. The result was fruit from the witness of the believers so that the churches increased in number daily (see 2:47). It was certainly a most successful tour, but I wonder if any of the believers asked about Barnabas? And what did Paul tell them?

Perhaps the best thing that happened at Lystra was the enlistment of Timothy to replace John Mark as Paul's special assistant. Timothy was probably converted through Paul's ministry when the apostle first visited Lystra, for Paul called him "my beloved son" (1 Cor. 4:17) and "my own son in the faith" (1 Tim. 1:2). Timothy's mother and grandmother had prepared the way for his decision by being the first in the family to trust Christ (2 Tim. 1:5). Young Timothy undoubtedly witnessed Paul's sufferings in Lystra (Acts 14:19-20;

2 Tim. 3:10-11) and was drawn by the Lord to the apostle. Timothy was Paul's favorite companion and coworker (Phil. 2:19-23), perhaps the son Paul never had but always wanted.

Because he had a good report from the churches (1 Tim. 3:7), Timothy was ordained by Paul and added to his "team" (1 Tim. 4:14; 2 Tim. 1:6). Paul's next step was to have Timothy circumcised, an action that seems to contradict the decision of the Jerusalem conference. However, there was an important spiritual principle behind Paul's decision.

The decision at the Jerusalem conference was that it was not necessary to be circumcised *in order to be saved*. Paul did not allow Titus to be circumcised lest the enemy think he was promoting their cause (Gal. 2:1-5). The battle in Jerusalem was over the truth of the Gospel, not over the fitness of a man to serve. Paul's concern with Timothy was not his salvation but his fitness for service.

Timothy would be working with both Jews and Gentiles in the churches, and it was essential that he not offend them. That was why Paul had Timothy circumcised (see 1 Cor. 9:19-23). Again, it was not a matter of Timothy's salvation or personal character, but rather of avoiding serious problems that would surely become stumbling blocks as the men sought to serve the Lord (Rom. 14:13-15). It is a wise spiritual leader who knows how and when to apply the principles of the Word of God, when to stand firm and when to yield.

In the years that followed, Timothy played an important part in the expansion and strengthening of the churches. He traveled with Paul and was often his special ambassador to the "trouble spots" in the work, such as Corinth. He became shepherd of the church in Ephesus (1 Tim. 1:3) and probably joined Paul in Rome shortly before the apostle was martyred (2 Tim. 4:21).

3. A New Vision (16:6-40)

In this section, we see three wonderful "openings."

God opened the way (vv. 6-12). After visiting the churches he had founded, Paul tried to enter new territory for the Lord by traveling east into Asia Minor and Bythinia, but the Lord closed the door. We don't know how God revealed His will in this matter, but we can well imagine that Paul was disappointed and perhaps a bit discouraged. Everything had been going so smoothly on this second journey that these closed doors must have come as a great surprise. However, it is comforting to know that even apostles were not always clear as to God's will for their ministries! God planned for the message to get there another time (18:19–19:41; and see 1 Peter 1:1).

In His sovereign grace, God led Paul west into Europe, not east into Asia. It is interesting to speculate how world history might have been changed had Paul been sent to Asia instead of to Europe. At Troas, Paul was called to Macedonia by a man whom he saw in a night vision. "Nothing makes a man strong like a call for help," wrote George MacDonald, and Paul was quick to respond to the vision (compare 26:19).

Note the pronoun *we* in verse 10, for Dr. Luke, who wrote the Book of Acts, joined Paul and his party at Troas. There are three "we sections" in Acts: 16:10-17; 20:5-15; and 27:1–28:16. Luke changed from "we" to "they" in 17:1, which suggests that he may have remained in Philippi to pastor the church after Paul left. The next "we section" begins in 20:5 in connection with Paul's trip from Macedonia. Luke devoted a good deal of space to Paul's ministry in Philippi, so perhaps he was a resident of that city. Some students think Luke may have been the man Paul saw in the vision.

From Troas to Neapolis, the port of Philippi was a distance of about 150 miles, and it took them two days to make the journey. Later, the trip in the opposite direction would take five days, apparently because of contrary winds (20:6). Philippi lay ten miles inland from Neapolis, and the way Luke described the city would suggest that he was indeed one of its proudest citizens.

Philippi was a Roman colony, which meant that it was a "Rome away from Rome." The emperor organized "colonies" by ordering Roman citizens, especially retired military people, to live in selected places so there would be strong pro-Roman cities in these strategic areas. Though living on foreign soil, the citizens were expected to be loyal to Rome, to obey the laws of Rome, and to give honor to the Roman emperor. In return, they were given certain political privileges, not the least of which was exemption from taxes. This was their reward for leaving their homes in Italy and relocating elsewhere.

God opened Lydia's heart (vv. 13-15). Paul and his friends did not plunge immediately into evangelizing the city, even though they knew God had called them there. No doubt they needed to rest and pray and make their plans together. It is not enough to know *where* God wants us to work; we must also know *when* and *how* He wants us to work.

The Jewish population in Philippi must have been very small since there was no synagogue there, only a place of prayer by the river outside the city. (It required ten men for the founding of a synagogue.) Paul had seen a *man* in the vision at Troas, but here he was ministering to a group of *women!* "It is better that the words of the Law be burned than be delivered to a woman!" said the rabbis; but that was no longer Paul's philosophy. He had been obedient and the Lord had gone before to prepare the way.

Lydia was a successful businesswoman from Thyatira, a city renowned for its purple dye. She probably was in charge of a branch office of her guild in Philippi. God brought her all the way to Greece so that she might hear the Gospel and be converted. She was "a worshiper of God," a Gentile who was not a full Jewish proselyte but who openly worshiped with the Jews. She was seeking truth.

Paul shared the Word ("spoken" in v. 14 means personal conversation, not preaching), God opened her heart to the truth, and she believed and was saved. She boldly identified herself with Christ by being baptized, and she insisted that the missionaries stay at her house. All of her household had been converted, so this was a good opportunity for Paul and his associates to teach them the Word and establish a local church. (We will deal with "household salvation" when we get to v. 31.)

We must not conclude that because *God* opened Lydia's heart, Lydia's part in her conversion was entirely passive. She listened attentively to the Word, and it is the Word that brings the sinner to the Saviour (John 5:24). The same God who ordained the end, Lydia's salvation, also ordained the *means to the end*, Paul's witness of Jesus Christ. This is a beautiful illustration of 2 Thessalonians 2:13-14.

God opened the prison doors (vv. 16-40). No sooner are lost people saved than Satan begins to hinder the work. In this case, he used a demonized girl who had made her masters wealthy by telling fortunes. As Paul and his "team" went regularly to the place of prayer, still witnessing to the lost, this girl repeatedly shouted after them, "These men are the servants of the Most High God, who show us the way of salvation!" Paul did not want either the Gospel or the name of God to be "promoted" by one of Satan's slaves, so he cast out the demon. After all, Satan may speak the truth one minute and the next minute tell a lie; and the unsaved would not know the difference.

The owners had no concern for the girl; they were interested only in the income she provided, and now that income was gone. (The conflict between money and ministry appears often in Acts: 5:1-11; 8:18-24; 19:23ff; 20:33-34.) Their only recourse was the Roman law, and they thought they had a pretty good case because the missionaries were Jewish and were propagating a religion not approved by Rome. Moved by both religious and racial prejudices, the magistrates acted rashly and did not investigate the matter fully. This neglect on their part later brought them embarrassment.

Why didn't Paul and Silas plead their Roman citizenship? (see 22:25-29; 25:11-12) Perhaps there was not time, or perhaps Paul was saving that weapon for better use later on. He and Silas were stripped and beaten (see 2 Cor. 11:23, 25) and put in the city prison. It looked like the end of their witness in Philippi, but God had other plans.

Instead of complaining or calling on God to judge their enemies, the two men prayed and praised God. When you are in pain, the midnight hour is not the easiest time for a sacred concert, but God gives "songs in the night" (Job 35:10; also see Ps. 42:8). "Any fool can sing in the day," said Charles Haddon Spurgeon. "It is easy to sing when we can read the notes by daylight; but the skillful singer is he who can sing when there is not a ray of light to read by. . . . Songs in the night come only from God; they are not in the power of men."

Prayer and praise are powerful weapons (2 Chron. 20:1-22; Acts 4:23-37). God responded by shaking the foundations of the prison, opening all the doors, and loosening the prisoners' bonds. They could have fled to freedom, but instead they remained right where they were. For one thing, Paul immediately took command; and, no doubt, the fear of God was upon these pagan men. The prisoners must have realized that there was something very special about those two Jewish preachers!

Paul's attention was fixed on the jailer, the man he really wanted to win to Christ. It was a Roman law that if a guard lost a prisoner, he was given the same punishment the prisoner would have received; so there must have been some men in the prison who had committed capital crimes. The jailer would rather commit suicide than face shame and execution. A hard-hearted person seeking vengeance would have let the cruel jailer kill himself, but Paul was not that kind of a man (see Matt. 5:10-12, 43-48). It was the jailer who was the prisoner, not Paul; and Paul not only saved the man's life, but pointed him to eternal life in Christ.

"What must I do to be saved?" is the cry of lost people worldwide, and we had better be able to give them the right answer. The legalists in the church would have replied, "Unless you are circumcised according to the custom of Moses, you cannot be saved" (15:1, NKJV). But Paul knew the right answer—faith in Jesus Christ. In the Book of Acts, the emphasis is on faith in Jesus Christ alone (2:38-39; 4:12; 8:12, 37; 10:10-43; 13:38-39).

The phrase "and thy house" does not mean that the faith of the jailer would automatically bring salvation to his family. Each sinner must trust Christ personally in order to be born again, for we cannot be saved "by proxy." The phrase means "and your household will be saved if they will also believe." We must not read into this statement the salvation of infants (with or without baptism) because it is clear that Paul was dealing with people old enough to hear the Word (v. 32), to believe and to rejoice (v. 34).

So-called "household salvation" has no basis in the Word of God—that is, that the decision of the head of the household brings salvation to the members of the household. The people in the household of Cornelius were old enough to respond to his call (10:24) and to understand the Word and believe (10:44; 11:15-17; 15:7-9). The household of Crispus was composed of people old enough to hear and believe God's Word (18:8). There is no suggestion here that the adults made decisions for infants or children.

It is touching to see the change in the attitude of the jailer as he washed the wounds of these two prisoners who were now his brothers in Christ. One of the evidences of true repentance is a loving desire to make restitution and reparation wherever we have hurt others. We should not only wash one another's feet (John 13:14-15), but we should also cleanse the wounds we have given to others.

What about the other prisoners? Luke doesn't give us the details, but it is possible that some of them were also born again through the witness of Paul and Silas and the jailer. Some of these prisoners may have been waiting for execution, so imagine their joy at hearing a message of salvation! Paul and Silas thought nothing of their own pains as they rejoiced in what God did in that Philippian jail! No doubt the jailer later joined with Lydia in the assembly.

The city officials knew that they had no convincing case against Paul and Silas, so they sent word to the jailer to release them. Paul, however, was unwilling to "sneak out of town," for that kind of exit would have left the new church under a cloud of suspicion. People would have asked, "Who were those men? Were they guilty of some crime? Why did they leave so quickly? What do their followers believe?" Paul and his associates wanted to leave behind a strong witness of their own integrity as well as a good testimony for the infant church in Philippi.

It was then that Paul made use of his Roman citizenship and boldly challenged the officials on the legality of their treatment. This was not personal revenge but a desire to give protection and respect for the church. While the record does not say that the magistrates officially and publicly apologized, it does state that they respectfully came to Paul and Silas, escorted them out of the prison, and politely asked them to leave town. Paul and Silas remained in Philippi long enough to visit the new believers and encourage them in the Lord.

As you review this chapter, you can see that the work of the

Lord progresses through difficulties and challenges. Sometimes the workers have problems with each other, and sometimes the problems come from the outside. It is also worth noting that not every sinner comes to Christ in exactly the same manner. Timothy was saved partly through the influence of a godly mother and grandmother. Lydia was converted through a quiet conversation with Paul at a Jewish prayer meeting, while the jailer's conversion was dramatic. One minute he was a potential suicide, and the next minute he was a child of God!

Different people with different experiences, and yet all of them changed by the grace of God.

Others just like them are waiting to be told God's simple plan of salvation.

Will you help them hear?

In your own witness for Christ, will you be daring?

4

Responding to God's Word

Acts 17

This chapter describes Paul's ministry in three cities and how some of the people in those cities responded to the Word of God. These pictures are snapshots, not murals, for Dr. Luke did not give us many details. However, as we study these three different responses, we can certainly see our modern world and better understand what to expect as we seek to witness for Christ today.

1. Thessalonica: Resisting the Word (17:1-9)

Following the famous Egnatian Way, Paul and Silas went 100 miles from Philippi to Thessalonica. (Timothy is not mentioned again until 17:14, so he may have remained in Philippi.) As far as we can tell, they did not pause to minister in either Amphipolis or Apollonia. Perhaps there were no synagogues in those cities, and Paul certainly expected the new believers in Philippi to carry the message to their neighbors. It was Paul's policy to minister in the larger cities and make them centers for evangelizing a whole district (see 19:10, 26; and 1 Thes. 1:8).

Paul knew that Thessalonica (our modern Salonika) was a strategic city for the work of the Lord. Not only was it the capital of Macedonia, but it was also a center for business, rivaled only by Corinth. It was located on several important trade routes, and it boasted an excellent harbor. The city was predominantly Greek, even though it was controlled by Rome. Thessalonica was a "free city," which meant that it had an elected citizens' assembly, it could mint its own coins, and it had no Roman garrison within its walls.

Paul labored at his tentmaking trade (Acts 18:3; 1 Thes. 2:9; 2 Thes. 3:7-10), but on the Sabbath ministered in the Jewish synagogue where he knew he would find both devout Jews and Gentiles, "God-seekers" and proselytes. This witness went on for only three Sabbaths; then he had to minister outside the synagogue. We do not know exactly how long Paul remained in Thessalonica, but it was long enough to receive financial help twice from the church in Philippi (Phil. 4:15-16). Read 1 Thessalonians 1 to learn how God blessed Paul's ministry and how the message spread from Thessalonica to other places. It was not a long ministry, but it was an effective one.

Four key words in verses 2-3 describe Paul's approach to the synagogue congregation. First, he *reasoned*, which means he dialogued with them through questions and answers. He *explained* ("opening") the Scriptures to them and *proved* ("alleging") that Jesus is indeed the Messiah. The word translated "alleging" means "to lay down alongside, to prove by presenting the evidence." The apostle set before them one Old Testament proof after another that Jesus of Nazareth is Messiah God.

Paul was careful to *announce* ("preach") the death and resurrection of Jesus Christ, which is the message of the Gospel (1 Cor. 15:1ff). In the sermons in Acts, you will find an emphasis on the resurrection, for the believers were called to

be witnesses of His resurrection (1:21-22; 2:32; 3:15; 5:32).
"Christianity is in its very essence a resurrection religion,"
says Dr. John R.W. Stott. "The concept of resurrection lies at
its heart. If you remove it, Christianity is destroyed."

As the result of three weeks' ministry, Paul saw a large
number of people believe, especially Greek proselytes and influential women. Among the men were Aristarchus and Se-
cundus, who later traveled with Paul (20:4). Luke's phrase
"not a few" (vv. 4, 12) is one way of saying, "It was a big
crowd!"

But these results did not bring joy to everybody. The unbelieving Jews envied Paul's success and were grieved to see the
Gentiles and the influential women leaving the synagogue.
Paul hoped that the salvation of the Gentiles would "provoke"
the Jews into studying the Scriptures and discovering their
promised Messiah (Rom. 11:13-14), but in this case, it only
provoked them into persecuting the infant church.

The Jews wanted to drag the missionaries before their city
assembly ("the people," v. 5, and see 19:30), so they manufactured a riot to get the attention of the magistrates. Unable to
find the missionaries, the mob seized Jason, host to Paul and
his friends, and took him and some of the believers instead.
The Jews' accusations were similar to the ones used at the
trial of Jesus: disturbing the peace and promoting treason
(Luke 23:2). Their crime was that of "saying that there is
another king, one Jesus."

The Greek word translated *another* means "another of a
different kind," that is, a king unlike Caesar. When you read
Paul's two Thessalonian letters, you see the strong emphasis
he gave in Thessalonica on the kingship of Christ and the
promise of His return. Of course, our Lord's kingdom is neither political nor "of this world" (John 18:36-37), but we
cannot expect unsaved pagans to understand this.

The kingship of Jesus Christ is unlike that of the rulers of this world. He conquers with ambassadors, not armies; and His weapons are truth and love. He brings men peace by upsetting the peace and turning things upside down! He conquers through His cross where He died for a world of lost sinners. He even died for His enemies! (Rom. 5:6-10)

The mob was agitated because they could not find Paul and Silas, so they settled for second best and obtained a peace bond against them. Jason had to put up the money and guarantee that Paul and Silas would leave the city and not return. It is possible that Jason was a relative of Paul's, which would make the transaction even more meaningful (Rom. 16:21). Paul saw this prohibition as a device of Satan to hinder the work (1 Thes. 2:18), but it certainly did not hinder the Thessalonian church from "sounding out the word" and winning the lost (1 Thes. 1:6-9).

2. Berea: Receiving the Word (17:10-15)

Under cover of night, Paul and Silas left the city and headed for Berea, about forty-five miles away. It does not appear that Timothy was with them, as he was probably working in Philippi. Later, he would join Paul in Athens (v. 15) and then be sent to Thessalonica to encourage the church in its time of persecution (1 Thes. 3:1ff). Since Timothy was a Gentile, and had not been present when the trouble erupted, he could minister in the city freely. The peace bond could keep Paul out, but it would not apply to Paul's young assistant.

Paul went into the synagogue and there discovered a group of people keenly interested in the study of the Old Testament Scriptures. In fact, they met *daily* to search the Scriptures to determine whether or not what Paul was saying was true. Paul had been overjoyed at the way the people in Thessalonica had received the Word (1 Thes. 2:13), so these "noble Bereans" must have really encouraged his heart. All of us should imitate these Bereans by faithfully studying God's

Word daily, discussing it, and testing the messages that we hear.

God used His Word so that many people trusted Christ. One of the men who was converted was Sopater, who later assisted Paul (20:4). He may be the same man (Sosipater) who later sent greetings to the Christians in Rome (Rom. 16:21).

Once again, Satan brought the enemy to the field as the unbelieving Jews from Thessalonica came to Berea and stirred up the people. (Note 1 Thes. 2:13-20.) How did these men hear that Paul and Silas were ministering in Berea? Perhaps the growing witness of the Berean believers reached as far as Thessalonica, or it may be that some troublemaker took the message to his friends in Thessalonica. Satan also has his "missionaries" and they are busy (2 Cor. 11:13-15).

The believers in Berea outwitted the enemy by taking Paul to the sea and putting him on a ship bound for Athens. Once more, Paul had to leave a place of rich ministry and break away from dear people he had come to love. Silas and Timothy later joined Paul in Athens, and then Timothy was sent to Thessalonica to help the saints there (1 Thes. 3:1-6). Silas was also sent on a special mission somewhere in Macedonia (Philippi?), and later both men met Paul in Corinth (18:1-5).

3. Athens: Ridiculing the Word (17:16-34)

Paul arrived in the great city of Athens, not as a sightseer, but as a soul-winner. The late Noel O. Lyons, for many years director of the Greater Europe Mission, used to say, "Europe is looked over by millions of visitors and is overlooked by millions of Christians." Europe needs the Gospel today just as it did in Paul's day, and we dare not miss our opportunities. Like Paul, we must have open eyes and broken hearts.

The City. Athens was in a period of decline at this time,

though still recognized as a center of culture and education. The glory of its politics and commerce had long since faded. It had a famous university and numerous beautiful buildings, but it was not the influential city it once had been. The city was given over to a "cultured paganism" that was nourished by idolatry, novelty (v. 21), and philosophy.

"The Greek religion was a mere deification of human attributes and the powers of nature," wrote Conybeare and Howson in their classic *Life and Epistles of St. Paul.* "It was a religion which ministered to art and amusement, and was entirely destitute of moral power" (pp. 280-281). The Greek myths spoke of gods and goddesses that, in their own rivalries and ambitions, acted more like humans than gods; and there were plenty of deities to choose from! One wit jested that in Athens it was easier to find a god than a man. Paul saw that the city was "wholly given to idolatry," and it broke his heart.

We today admire Greek sculpture and architecture as beautiful works of art, but in Paul's day, much of this was directly associated with their religion. Paul knew that idolatry was demonic (1 Cor. 10:14-23) and that the many gods of the Greeks were only characters in stories who were unable to change men's lives (1 Cor. 8:1-6). With all of their culture and wisdom, the Greeks did not know the true God (1 Cor. 1:18-25).

As for novelty, it was the chief pursuit of both the citizens and the visitors (v. 21). Their leisure time was spent telling or hearing "some new thing." Eric Hoffer wrote that "the fear of becoming a 'has been' keeps some people from becoming anything." The person who chases the new and ignores the old soon discovers that he has no deep roots to nourish his life. He also discovers that nothing is really new; it's just that our memories are poor (Ecc. 1:8-11).

The city was also devoted to philosophy. When you think of Greece, you automatically think of Socrates and Aristotle and a host of other thinkers whose works are still read and studied today. Newspaper columnist Franklin P. Adams once defined philosophy as "unintelligible answers to insoluble problems," but the Greeks would not have agreed with him. They would have followed Aristotle who called philosophy "the science which considers truth."

Paul had to confront two opposing philosophies as he witnessed in Athens, those of the Epicureans and the Stoics. We today associate the word *Epicurean* with the pursuit of pleasure and the love of "fine living," especially fine food. But the Epicurean philosophy involved much more than that. In one sense, the founder Epicurus was an "existentialist" in that he sought truth by means of personal experience and not through reasoning. The Epicureans were materialists and atheists, and their goal in life was pleasure. To some, "pleasure" meant that which was grossly physical; but to others, it meant a life of refined serenity, free from pain and anxiety. The true Epicurean avoided extremes and sought to enjoy life by keeping things in balance, but pleasure was still his number one goal.

The Stoics rejected the idolatry of pagan worship and taught that there was one "World God." They were pantheists, and their emphasis was on personal discipline and self-control. Pleasure was not good and pain was not evil. The most important thing in life was to follow one's reason and be self-sufficient, unmoved by inner feelings or outward circumstances. Of course, such a philosophy only fanned the flames of pride and taught men that they did not need the help of God. It is interesting that the first two leaders of the Stoic school committed suicide.

The Epicureans said "Enjoy life!" and the Stoics said "Endure life!" but it remained for Paul to explain how they could enter into life through faith in God's risen Son.

The Witness. "Left at Athens alone" (1 Thes. 3:1), Paul

viewed the idolatrous city and his spirit was "stirred" (same word as "contention" in 15:39—"paroxysm"). Therefore, he used what opportunities were available to share the good news of the Gospel. As was his custom, he "dialogued" in the synagogue with the Jews, but he also witnessed in the market-place (agora) to the Greeks. Anyone who was willing to talk was welcomed by Paul to his daily "classes."

It did not take long for the philosophers to hear about this "new thing" that was going on in the *agora*, and they came and listened to Paul and probably debated with him. As they listened, they gave two different responses. One group ridiculed Paul and his teachings and called him a "babbler." The word literally means "birds picking up seed," and it refers to someone who collects various ideas and teaches as his own the secondhand thoughts he borrows from others. It was not a very flattering description of the church's greatest missionary and theologian.

The second group was confused but interested. They thought Paul believed as they themselves did in many gods, because he was preaching "Jesus and Anastasis" (the Greek word for "resurrection"). The word translated "preached" in verse 18 means "to preach the Gospel." Those who say that Paul modified his evangelistic tactics in Athens, hoping to appeal to the intellectuals, have missed the point. He preached the Gospel as boldly in Athens as he did in Berea and would do in Corinth.

The Defense. The Council of the Aeropagus was responsible to watch over both religion and education in the city, so it was natural for them to investigate the "new doctrine" Paul was teaching. They courteously invited Paul to present his doctrine at what appears to have been an informal meeting of the council on Mars' Hill. Paul was not on trial; the council members only wanted him to explain what he had been telling the people in the *agora*. After all, life in Athens consisted in hearing and telling new things, and Paul had something new!

Paul's message is a masterpiece of communication. He started where the people were by referring to their altar dedicated to an unknown god. Having aroused their interest, he then explained who that God was and what He is like. He concluded the message with a personal application that left each council member facing a moral decision, and some of them decided for Jesus Christ.

Paul opened his address with a compliment: "I see that in every way you are very religious" (v. 22, NIV). They were so religious, in fact, that they even had an altar to "the unknown god," lest some beneficent deity be neglected. If they did not know this god, how could they worship him? Or how could he help them? It was this God that Paul declared.

In this message, which is similar to his sermon at Lystra (14:15-17), Paul shared four basic truths about God.

(1) *The greatness of God: He is Creator* (v. 24). Every thinking person asks, "Where did I come from? Why am I here? Where am I going?" Science attempts to answer the first question, and philosophy wrestles with the second; but only the Christian faith has a satisfactory answer to all three. The Epicureans, who were atheists, said that all was matter and matter always was. The Stoics said that everything was God, "the Spirit of the Universe." God did not create anything; He only organized matter and impressed on it some "law and order."

But Paul boldly affirmed, "In the beginning, God!" God made the world and everything in it, and He is Lord of all that He has made. He is not a distant God, divorced from His creation; nor is He an imprisoned God, locked in creation. He is too great to be housed in man-made temples (1 Kings 8:27; Isa. 66:1-2; Acts 7:48-50), but He is not too great to be concerned about man's needs (v. 25). We wonder how the Council members reacted to Paul's statement about temples, for right there on the Acropolis were several shrines dedicated to Athena.

(2) *The goodness of God; He is Provider* (v. 25). Men may pride themselves in serving God, but it is God who serves man. If God is God, then He is self-sufficient and needs nothing that man can supply. Not only do the temples not contain God, but the services in the temples add nothing to God! In two brief statements, Paul completely wiped out the entire religious system of Greece!

It is God who gives to us what we need: " . . . life, and breath, and all things." God is the source of every good and perfect gift (James 1:17). He gave us life and He sustains that life by His goodness (Matt. 5:45). It is the goodness of God that should lead men to repentance (Rom. 2:4). But instead of worshiping the Creator and glorifying Him, men worship His creation and glorify themselves (Rom. 1:18-25).

(3) *The government of God: He is Ruler* (vv. 26-29). The gods of the Greeks were distant beings who had no concern for the problems and needs of men. But the God of Creation is also the God of history and geography! He created mankind "from one man" (v. 36, NIV) so that all nations are made of the same stuff and have the same blood. The Greeks felt that they were a special race, different from other nations; but Paul affirmed otherwise. Even their precious land that they revered came as a gift from God. It is not the power of man, but the government of God, that determines the rise and fall of nations (Dan. 4:35).

God is not a distant deity; "He [is] not far from every one of us" (v. 27). Therefore, men ought to seek God and come to know Him in truth. Here Paul quoted from the poet Epimenides: "For in Him we live, and move, and have our being." Then he added a quotation from two poets, Aratus and Cleanthes, "For we are also His offspring." Paul was not saying that all people on earth are the spiritual children of God, for sinners become God's children only by faith in Jesus Christ (John 1:11-13). Rather, he was affirming the "Fatherhood of God" in a *natural* sense, for man was created in the image of God (Gen. 1:26). In this sense, Adam was a "son of God" (Luke 3:38).

This led to Paul's logical conclusion: God made us in His image, so it is foolish for us to make gods in our own image! Greek religion was nothing but the manufacture and worship of gods who were patterned after men and who acted like men. Paul not only showed the folly of temples and the temple rituals, but also the folly of all idolatry.

(4) *The grace of God: He is Saviour* (vv. 30-31). As he brought his message to a close, Paul summarized the clear evidences of God's grace. For centuries, God was patient with man's sin and ignorance (see 14:16 and Rom. 3:25). This does not mean that men were not guilty (Rom. 1:19-20), but only that God held back divine wrath. In due time, God sent a Saviour, and now He commands all men to repent of their foolish ways. This Saviour was killed and then raised from the dead, and one day, He will return to judge the world. The proof that He will judge is that He was raised from the dead.

It was the doctrine of the resurrection that most of the members of the Council could not accept. To a Greek, the body was only a prison; and the sooner a person left his body, the happier he would be. Why raise a dead body and live in it again? And why would God bother with a personal judgment of each man? This kind of teaching was definitely incompatible with Greek philosophy. They believed in immortality, but not in resurrection.

There were three different responses to the message. Some laughed and mocked and did not take Paul's message seriously. Others were interested but wanted to hear more. A small group accepted what Paul preached, believed on Jesus Christ, and were saved. We wonder if the others who postponed their decision eventually trusted Christ. We hope they did.

When you contrast the seeming meager results in Athens with the great harvests in Thessalonica and Berea, you are tempted to conclude that Paul's ministry there was a dismal failure. If you do, you might find yourself drawing a hasty and erroneous conclusion. Paul was not told to leave, so we assume he lingered in Athens and continued to minister to both believers and unbelievers. Proud, sophisticated, wise Athens would not take easily to Paul's humbling message of the Gospel, especially when he summarized all of Greek history in the phrase "the times of this ignorance." The soil here was not deep and it contained many weeds, but there was a small harvest.

And, after all, one soul is worth the whole world!

We still need witnesses who will invade the "halls of academe" and present Christ to people who are wise in this world but ignorant of the true wisdom of the world to come. "Not many wise men after the flesh, not many mighty, not many noble are called" (1 Cor. 1:26); but some *are* called, and God may use you to call them.

Take the Gospel to your "Athens." Be daring!

5

It's Always Too Soon to Quit

Acts 18:1-22

A man was shoveling snow from his driveway when two boys carrying snow shovels approached him.

"Shovel your snow, Mister?" one of them asked. "Only two dollars!"

Puzzled, the man replied, "Can't you see that I'm doing it myself?"

"Sure," said the enterprising lad; "that's why we asked. We get most of our business from people who are half through and feel like quitting!"

Dr. V. Raymond Edman used to say to the students at Wheaton (Illinois) College, "It's always too soon to quit!" And Charles Spurgeon reminded his London congregation, "By perseverance, the snail reached the ark."

Corinth, with its 200,000 people, would not be the easiest city in which to start a church, and yet that's where Paul went after leaving Athens. And he went alone! The going was tough, but the apostle did not give up.

Corinth's reputation for wickedness was known all over the Roman Empire. (Rom. 1:18-32 was written in Corinth!)

Thanks to its location, the city was a center for both trade and travel. Money and vice, along with strange philosophies and new religions, came to Corinth and found a home there. Corinth was the capital of Achaia and one of the two most important cities Paul visited. The other was Ephesus.

When God opens doors, the enemy tries to close them, and there are times when we close the doors on ourselves because we get discouraged and quit. As Paul ministered in Corinth, the Lord gave him just the encouragements that he needed to keep him going, and these same encouragements are available to us today.

1. Devoted Helpers (18:1-5)

Paul came to Corinth following his ministry to the philosophers in Greece; and he determined to magnify Jesus Christ and the cross, to depend on the Holy Spirit, and to present the Gospel in simplicity (1 Cor. 2:1-5). There were many philosophers and itinerant teachers in Corinth, preying on the ignorant and superstitious population; and Paul's message and ministry could easily be misunderstood.

One way Paul separated himself from the "religious hucksters" was by supporting himself as a tentmaker. By the providence of God, he met a Jewish couple, Aquila and Priscilla (Prisca, 2 Tim. 4:19), who were workers in leather as was Paul. Jewish rabbis did not accept money from their students but earned their way by practicing a trade. All Jewish boys were expected to learn a trade, no matter what profession they might enter. "He who does not teach his son to work, teaches him to steal!" said the rabbis; so Saul of Tarsus learned to make leather tents and to support himself in his ministry. (See Acts 18:3; 1 Cor. 9:6-15; 2 Cor. 11:6-10.)

Were Aquila and Priscilla Christian believers at that time? We don't know for certain, but it's likely that they were. Perhaps they were even founding members of the church in

Rome. We do know that this dedicated couple served most faithfully and even risked their lives for Paul (Rom. 16:3-4). They assisted him in Ephesus (18:18-28) where they even hosted a church in their home (1 Cor. 16:19). Aquila and Priscilla were an important part of Paul's "team" and he thanked God for them. They are a good example of how "lay ministers" can help to further the work of the Lord. Every pastor and missionary thanks God for people like Aquila and Priscilla, people with hands, hearts, and homes dedicated to the work of the Lord.

Paul lived and worked with Aquila and Priscilla, but on the Sabbath days witnessed boldly in the synagogue. After all, that was why he had come to Corinth. When Silas and Timothy arrived from Macedonia (17:14-15; 18:5), they brought financial aid (2 Cor. 11:9), and this enabled Paul to devote his full time to the preaching of the Gospel. What a joy it must have been for Paul to see his friends and to hear from them the good news of the steadfastness of the Christians in the churches they had planted together (1 Thes. 3).

Everyone agrees that Paul was a great Christian and a great missionary evangelist, but how much would Paul have accomplished *alone?* Friends like Aquila and Priscilla, Silas and Timothy, and the generous believers in Macedonia, made it possible for Paul to serve the Lord effectively. His Christian friends, new and old, encouraged him at a time when he needed it the most.

Of course, this reminds us that we should encourage our friends in the work of the Lord. Ralph Waldo Emerson wrote, "God evidently does not intend us all to be rich or powerful or great, but He does intend us all to be friends." "Bear ye one another's burdens, and so fulfill the law of Christ" is the way Paul expressed it (Gal. 6:2). Humanly speaking, there would have been no church in Corinth were it not for the devotion and service of many different people.

2. Opposition (18:6-8)

Whenever God is blessing a ministry, you can expect increased opposition as well as increased opportunities. "For a great and effective door has opened to me, and there are many adversaries" (1 Cor. 16:9, NKJV). After all, the enemy gets angry when we invade his territory and liberate his slaves. As in Thessalonica and Berea (17:5-13), the unbelieving Jews who rejected the Word stirred up trouble for Paul and his friends. (See 1 Thes. 2:14-16.) Such opposition is usually proof that God is at work, and this ought to encourage us. Spurgeon used to say that the devil never kicks a dead horse!

Jewish opposition had forced Paul to leave Thessalonica and Berea, but in Corinth, it only made him determined to stay there and get the job done. It is always too soon to quit! Like the undaunted Christopher Columbus, Paul could write in his journal, "Today we sailed on!"

Two interesting Old Testament images are found in verse 6. To shake out one's garments was an act of judgment that said, "You have had your opportunity, but now it's over!" Today we might say that we were washing our hands of a situation. (See Neh. 5:13, and compare Acts 13:51 and Matt. 10:14.) While Paul never ceased witnessing to the Jews, his primary calling was to evangelize the Gentiles (13:46-48; 28:28).

To have blood *on your hands* means that you bear the responsibility for another's death because you were not faithful to warn him. The image comes from the watchman on the city walls whose task it was to stay alert and warn of coming danger. (See Ezek. 3:17-21 and 33:1-9.) But to have blood *on your head* means that you are to blame for your own judgment. You had the opportunity to be saved, but you turned it down. (See Josh. 2:19.) Paul's hands were clean (Acts 20:26) because he had been faithful to declare the message of the

Gospel. The Jews had their own blood on their own heads because they rejected God's truth.

At just the right time, God brought another friend into Paul's life—Gentile, God-fearing Titus Justus. Some Bible students think his full name was Gaius Titus Justus and that he was the "Gaius my host" referred to in Romans 16:23. The connection between Gaius and Crispus in 18:7-8 and 1 Corinthians 1:14 is certainly significant.

Paul departed from the synagogue and began using the house of Titus Justus as his preaching station, right next to the synagogue! This was certainly a wise decision on Paul's part, because it gave him continued contact with the Jews and Gentile proselytes; and as a result, even the chief ruler of the synagogue was converted! It was the ruler's job to see to it that the synagogue building was cared for and that the services were held in a regular and orderly manner. We have here another instance of an entire family turning to the Lord (10:24, 44; 16:15, 34). How that must have stirred the Jewish population in Corinth!

When you examine Paul's ministry in Corinth, you will see that he was fulfilling the Lord's commission given in Matthew 28:19-20. Paul came to Corinth ("Go"), he won sinners to Christ ("make disciples"), he baptized, and he taught them (note v. 11). He even experienced the assurance of the Lord's "Lo, I am with thee always!" (vv. 9-10)

Paul's associates baptized most of the new converts (1 Cor. 1:11-17), just as our Lord's disciples did when He ministered on earth (John 4:1-2; and note Acts 10:46-48). The important thing is the believer's obedience to the Lord and not the name of the minister who does the baptizing. When I became senior pastor at the Moody Church in Chicago, an older member boastfully said to me, "I was baptized by Dr. Ironside!" He was surprised that I was not impressed. I was sure that Dr. Ironside would have lovingly rebuked him for speaking like that, for Dr. Ironside was a humble man who wanted Christ's name exalted, not his own.

To walk by faith means to see opportunities even in the midst of opposition. A pessimist sees only the problems; an optimist sees only the potential; but a realist sees the potential in the problems. Paul did not close his eyes to the many dangers and difficulties in the situation at Corinth, but he did look at them from the divine point of view.

Faith simply means obeying God's will in spite of feelings, circumstances, or consequences. There never was an easy place to serve God; and if there is an easy place, it is possible that something is wrong. Paul reminded Timothy, "Yes, and all who desire to live godly in Christ Jesus will suffer persecution" (2 Tim. 3:12, NKJV).

"Prosperity is the blessing of the Old Testament," wrote Francis Bacon; "adversity is the blessing of the New." Paul did not allow adversity to keep him from serving God.

3. The Word of Assurance (18:9-17)

The conversion of Crispus, an important Jewish leader, opened up more opportunities for evangelism and brought more opposition from the enemy! The Jewish community in Corinth was no doubt furious at Paul's success and did everything possible to silence him and get rid of him. Dr. Luke does not give us the details, but I get the impression that between verses 8 and 9, the situation became especially difficult and dangerous. Paul may have been thinking about leaving the city when the Lord came to him and gave him the assurance that he needed.

It is just like our Lord to speak to us when we need Him the most. His tender "Fear not!" can calm the storm in our hearts regardless of the circumstances around us. This is the way He assured Abraham (Gen. 15:1), Isaac (Gen. 26:24), and Jacob (Gen. 46:3), as well as Jehoshaphat (2 Chron. 20:15-17), Dan-

iel (Dan. 10:12, 19), Mary (Luke 1:30), and Peter (Luke 5:10).
The next time you feel alone and defeated, meditate on Hebrews 13:5 and Isaiah 41:10 and 43:1-7, and claim by faith
the presence of the Lord. He is with you!

When he was a young man, the famous British preacher
G. Campbell Morgan used to read the Bible each week to two
elderly women. One evening, when he finished reading the
closing words of Matthew 28, Morgan said to the ladies, "Isn't
that a wonderful promise!" and one of them replied, "Young
man, that is not a promise—it is a certainty!"

Jesus had already appeared to Paul on the Damascus road
(9:1-6; 26:12-18) and also in the temple (22:17-18). Paul
would be encouraged by Him again when he was imprisoned
in Jerusalem (23:11) and later in Rome (2 Tim. 4:16-17). Our
Lord's angel would also appear to Paul in the midst of the
storm and give him a word of assurance for the passengers
and crew (27:23-25). One of our Lord's names is "Immanu-
el—God with us" (Matt. 1:23), and He lives up to His name.

Paul was encouraged not only by the presence of the Lord,
but also by His promises. Jesus assured Paul that no one
would hurt him and that he would bring many sinners to the
Saviour. The statement "I have many people in this city" implies the doctrine of divine election, for "the Lord knows those
who are His" (2 Tim. 2:19, NKJV). God's church is made up of
people who were "chosen . . . in Him [Christ] before the
foundation of the world" (Eph. 1:4; and see Acts 13:48).

Please note that divine sovereignty in election is not a deter-
rent to human responsibility in evangelism. Quite the opposite
is true! Divine election is one of the greatest encouragements
to the preaching of the Gospel. Because Paul knew that God
already had people set apart for salvation, he stayed where he
was and preached the Gospel with faith and courage. Paul's
responsibility was to obey the commission; God's responsibility was to save sinners. If salvation depends on sinful man,

then all of our efforts are futile; but if "salvation is of the Lord" (Jonah 2:9), then we can expect Him to bless His Word and save souls.

"Scripture nowhere dispels the mystery of election," writes John Stott in *God's New Society* (InterVarsity, p. 37), "and we should beware of any who try to systematize it too precisely or rigidly. It is not likely that we shall discover a simple solution to a problem which has baffled the best brains of Christendom for centuries."

The important thing is that we accept God's truth and act upon it. Paul did not spend his time speculating about divine sovereignty and human responsibility, the way some ivory-tower Christians do today. *He got busy and tried to win souls to Christ!* You and I do not know who God's elect are, so we take the Gospel to every creature and let God do the rest. And we certainly do not discuss election with the lost! D.L. Moody once told some unconverted people, "You have no more to do with the doctrine of election than you have with the government of China!"

Before leaving this theme, we should note that it is our personal responsibility to make sure that we are among God's elect. "Therefore, brethren, be even more diligent to make your calling and election sure" (2 Peter 1:10, NKJV). To the inquisitive theorist who asked about the number of the elect, Jesus replied, "Strive to enter in at the narrow gate!" (Luke 13:23-24) In other words, "What you need is salvation for yourself, not speculation about others! Be sure you are saved yourself; then we can talk about these wonderful truths."

Paul continued in Corinth, knowing that God was with Him and that people would be saved. During those eighteen months of witness, Paul saw many victories in spite of Satan's opposition. The church was not made up of many mighty and noble people (1 Cor. 1:26-31), but of sinners whose lives were transformed by the grace of God (1 Cor. 6:9-11).

Dr. Luke shared only one example of divine protection during Paul's ministry in Corinth (vv. 12-17), but it is a significant one. The arrival of a new proconsul gave the unbelieving Jews hope that Rome might declare this new "Christian sect" illegal. They broke the law by attacking Paul and forcing him to go to court. This was not the first time that fanatical Jews had tried to prove that Paul was breaking the Roman law (16:19-24; 17:6-7).

Being a Roman citizen, Paul was prepared to defend himself; but this turned out to be unnecessary because Gallio defended Paul! The proconsul immediately saw that the real issue was not the application of the Roman law but the interpretation of the Jewish religion, so he refused to try the case!

But that was not the end of the matter. The Greeks who were witnessing the scene got hold of Sosthenes, the man who replaced Crispus as ruler of the synagogue, and beat him right before the eyes of the proconsul! It was certainly a flagrant display of anti-Semitism, but Gallio looked the other way. If this is the same Sosthenes mentioned by Paul in 1 Corinthians 1:1, then he too got converted; and the Jews had to find another ruler for their synagogue! It would be interesting to know exactly how it happened. Did Paul and some of the believers visit Sosthenes and minister to him? Perhaps his predecessor Crispus helped "wash the wounds" (16:33) and used this as an opportunity to share the love of Christ.

How strange and wonderful are the providences of God! The Jews tried to force the Roman proconsul to declare the Christian faith illegal, but Gallio ended up doing just the opposite. By refusing to try the case, Gallio made it clear that Rome would not get involved in cases involving Jewish religious disputes. As far as he was concerned, Paul and his disciples had as much right as the Jews to practice their religion and share it with others.

In the Book of Acts, Luke emphasizes the relationship between the Roman government and the Christian church. While it was true that the *Jewish* council prohibited the apostles to preach (4:17-21; 5:40), there is no evidence in Acts that Rome ever did so. In fact, in Philippi (16:35-40), Corinth, and Ephesus (19:31), the Roman officials were not only tolerant but almost cooperative. Paul knew how to use his Roman citizenship wisely so that the government worked for him and not against him, and he was careful not to accuse the government or try to escape its authority (25:10-12).

4. God's Will (18:18-22)

"If God will" (v. 21) was more than a religious slogan with Paul; it was one of the strengths and encouragements of his life and ministry. Knowing and doing God's will is one of the blessings of the Christian life (22:14). In some of his letters, Paul identified himself as "an apostle of Jesus Christ by the will of God" (1 Cor. 1:1; 2 Cor. 1:1; Eph. 1:1; Col. 1:1; 2 Tim. 1:1). At a most critical time in his life and ministry, Paul found courage in affirming, "The will of the Lord be done!" (21:14)

After eighteen months of ministry, Paul decided that it was God's will for him to leave Corinth and return to his home church in Antioch. His friends Priscilla and Aquila (note how Luke varies the order of their names) accompanied him to Ephesus and remained there when he departed for Caesarea. In verse 24, we will pick up the story of the church in Ephesus and the important part played by Aquila and Priscilla.

Cenchraea was the seaport for Corinth, and there was a Christian congregation there (Rom. 16:1). Here Paul had his head shorn, "for he had a vow." This probably refers to the Nazirite vow described in Numbers 6. Since the Nazirite vow was purely voluntary, Paul was not abandoning grace for law when he undertook it. The vow was not a matter of salvation but of personal devotion to the Lord. He allowed his hair to grow for a specific length of time and then cut it when the vow was completed. He also abstained from using the fruit of the vine in any form.

We are not told why Paul took this vow. Perhaps it was a part of his special dedication to God during the difficult days of the early ministry in Corinth. Or perhaps the vow was an expression of gratitude to God for all that He had done for him and his associates. According to Jewish law, the Nazirite vow had to be completed in Jerusalem with the offering of the proper sacrifices. The hair was shorn at the completion of the vow, not at the beginning; and it was not necessary for one to be in Jerusalem to make the vow.

Luke does not tell us how long Paul was in Ephesus, but the time was evidently very short. The Jews there were much more receptive to the Gospel and wanted Paul to stay; but he wanted to get to Jerusalem to complete his vow, and then to Antioch to report to the church. However, he did promise to return, and he kept that promise (19:1).

The statement "I must by all means keep this feast that cometh in Jerusalem" (v. 21) must not be interpreted to mean that Paul and the early Christians felt obligated to observe the Jewish feasts (see 20:16). Being in Jerusalem during the important feasts (in this case, Passover) would give Paul opportunity to meet and witness to key Jewish leaders from throughout the Roman Empire. He would also be able to minister to Christian Jews who returned to their homeland.

Paul taught clearly that the observing of religious feasts was neither a means of salvation nor an essential for sanctification (Gal. 4:1-11). Christians are at liberty to follow their own conscience so long as they do not judge others or cause others to stumble (Rom. 14:1–15:7). Also, keep in mind Paul's personal policy with regard to these matters of Jewish practice (1 Cor. 9:19-23).

Arriving at Caesarea, Paul went up to Jerusalem and greeted the believers there. He then went to Antioch and reported to his home church all that God had done on this second missionary journey. He had been gone from Antioch perhaps two years or more, and the saints were no doubt overjoyed to see him and hear about the work of God among the Gentiles.

There's no proof, but likely Paul kept reminding the believers in Antioch, "It's always too soon to quit!"

That's a good reminder for us to heed today.

6

Excitement in Ephesus

Acts 18:23–19:41

We don't know how long Paul remained in Antioch before leaving on his third missionary journey, but perhaps it was as long as a year. As in his second journey, he visited the churches and strengthened the believers. Luke does not describe this journey in detail because his main purpose is to get Paul to Ephesus. He wants to share with his readers the marvelous ministry God gave to Paul in that strategic city so steeped in idolatry and the occult.

Ephesus, with its 300,000 inhabitants, was the capital city of the Roman province of Asia and its most important commercial center. Thanks to a large harbor, Ephesus grew wealthy on trade; and, thanks to the temple of Diana, it attracted hosts of visitors who wanted to see this building that was one of the seven wonders of the world.

The temple was probably four centuries old in Paul's day. It measured 418 feet by 239 feet, and boasted of 100 columns that stood over 50 feet high. In the sacred enclosure of the temple stood the "sacred image" of Artemis (Diana) that was supposed to have fallen from heaven (19:35). It was probably a meteorite. Since Artemis was a fertility goddess, cultic prostitution was an important part of her worship, and hundreds of "priestesses" were available in the temple.

Paul's three years in Ephesus (20:31)—the longest he stayed in any city—were certainly exciting and fruitful. Let's meet some of the people who were involved.

1. A Man with an Incomplete Message (18:23-28)

When Paul departed from Ephesus for Jerusalem, he left his friends Aquila and Priscilla behind to carry on the witness in the synagogue. Imagine their surprise one Sabbath to hear a visiting Jewish teacher named Apollos preach many of the truths that they themselves believed and taught!

Apollos was certainly an exceptional man in many ways. He came from Alexandria, the second most important city in the Roman Empire. A center for education and philosophy, the city was founded by (and named after) Alexander the Great, and it boasted a university with a library of almost 700,000 volumes. The population of Alexandria (about 600,000) was quite cosmopolitan, being made up of Egyptians, Romans, Greeks, and Jews. At least a quarter of the population was Jewish, and the Jewish community was very influential.

Apollos knew the Old Testament Scriptures well and was able to teach them with eloquence and power. He was fervent ("boiling") in his spirit and diligent in his presentation of the message. He was bold enough to enter the synagogue and preach to the Jews. The only problem was that this enthusiastic man was declaring an incomplete Gospel. His message got as far as John the Baptist and then stopped! He knew nothing about Calvary, the resurrection of Christ, or the coming of the Holy Spirit at Pentecost. He had zeal, but he lacked spiritual knowledge (Rom. 10:1-4).

The ministry of John the Baptist was an important part of

God's redemptive plan. God sent John to prepare the nation of Israel for their Messiah (John 1:15-34). John's baptism was a baptism of repentance; those who were baptized looked forward to the coming Messiah (Acts 19:4). John also announced a future baptism of the Holy Spirit (Matt. 3:11; Mark 1:8) which took place on the Day of Pentecost (Acts 1:5). Apollos knew about the promises, but he did not know about their fulfillment.

Where did Apollos get his message to begin with? Since Alexandria was a famous center for learning, it is possible that some of John the Baptist's disciples (Matt. 14:12; Luke 11:1) had gone there while Christ was still ministering on earth, and shared with the Jews as much as they knew. The word *instructed* in 18:25 means "catechized" and suggests that Apollos had personal formal training in the Scriptures. However, that training was limited to the facts about the ministry of John the Baptist. Apollos' message was not inaccurate or insincere; it was just incomplete.

When I travel in conference ministry, I depend on my wife to plan the routes and do the navigating. (I can get lost in a parking lot!) On one particular trip, we got confused because we could not find a certain road. Then we discovered that our map was out of date! We quickly obtained a new map and everything was fine. Apollos had an old map that had been accurate in its day, but he desperately needed a new one. That new map was supplied by Aquila and Priscilla.

Aquila and Priscilla did not instruct him in public because that would have only confused the Jews. They took him home to a Sabbath dinner and then told him about Jesus Christ and the coming of the Holy Spirit. They led him into a deeper knowledge of Christ; and the next Sabbath, Apollos returned to the synagogue and gave the Jews the rest of the story! In fact, so effective was his ministry that the believers in Ephesus highly recommended him to the churches in Achaia. Here

Apollos not only strengthened the saints, but he also debated with the unbelieving Jews and convinced many of them that Jesus is the Messiah.

Apollos ministered for a time to the church in Corinth (19:1), where his learning and eloquence attracted attention (1 Cor. 1:12; 3:4-6, 22; 4:6). It is unfortunate that a clique gathered around him and helped bring division to the church, because he was definitely one of Paul's friends and a trusted helper (1 Cor. 16:12; Titus 3:13).

2. Twelve Men with an Inconsistent Witness (19:1-10)

When Paul arrived back in Ephesus, he met twelve men who professed to be Christian "disciples" but whose lives gave evidence that something was lacking. Paul asked them, "Did you receive the Holy Spirit when you believed?" (v. 2, NIV, NASB, NKJV) The question was important because *the witness of the Spirit is the one indispensable proof that a person is truly born again* (Rom. 8:9, 16; 1 John 5:9-13), and you receive the Spirit when you believe on Jesus Christ (Eph. 1:13).

Their reply revealed the vagueness and uncertainty of their faith, for they did not even know that the Holy Spirit had been given! As disciples of John the Baptist, they knew that there was a Holy Spirit, and that the Spirit would one day baptize God's people (Matt. 3:11; Luke 3:16; John 1:32-33). It is possible that these men were Apollos' early "converts" and therefore did not fully understand what Christ had done.

Why did Paul ask about their baptism? Because in the Book of Acts, a person's baptismal experience is an indication of his or her spiritual experience. Acts 1–10 records a transition period in the history of the church, from the apostles' ministry to the Jews to their ministry to the Gentiles. During this transition period, Peter uses "the keys of the kingdom" (Matt. 16:19) and opens the door of faith to the Jews (Acts 2), the Samaritans (Acts 8:14ff), and finally to the Gentiles (Acts 10).

It is important to note that God's pattern for today is given in Acts 10:43-48: sinners hear the Word, they believe on Jesus Christ, they *immediately* receive the Spirit, and then they are baptized. The Gentiles in Acts 10 did not receive the Spirit by means of water baptism or by the laying on of the apostles' hands (8:14-17).

The fact that these twelve men did not have the Spirit dwelling within was proof that they had never truly been born again. But they had been baptized by John's baptism, the same baptism that the apostles had received! (See Acts 1:21-22.) What was wrong with them?

Some people say that these men were already saved, but they lacked the fullness of the Spirit in their lives. So Paul explained how to be "baptized in the Spirit," and this led to a new life of victory. But that's not what the record says. Paul sensed that these men did not have the witness of the Spirit in their lives, and therefore they were not converted men. He certainly would not discuss the fullness of the Spirit with unsaved people! No, these twelve men had been baptized and were seeking to be religious, but something was missing. Alas, we have people just like them in our churches today!

Paul explained to them that John's baptism was a baptism of repentance that *looked forward* to the coming of the promised Messiah, while Christian baptism is a baptism that *looks back* to the finished work of Christ on the cross and His victorious resurrection. John's baptism was on "the other side" of Calvary and Pentecost. It was correct for its day, but now that day was ended.

Keep in mind that John the Baptist was a prophet who ministered under the old dispensation (Matt. 11:7-14). The old covenant was ended, not by John at the Jordan, but by Jesus Christ at Calvary (Heb. 10:1-18). The baptism of John was important to the Jews of that time (Matt. 21:23-32), but it is no longer valid for the church today. In a very real sense, these twelve men were like "Old Testament believers" who were anticipating the coming of the Messiah. Certainly Paul explained to the men many basic truths that Luke did not record. Then he baptized them, for their first "baptism" was not truly Christian baptism.

Why was it necessary for Paul to lay hands on these men before they could receive the Spirit? Didn't this contradict the experience of Peter recorded in Acts 10:44-48? Not if you keep in mind that this was a special group of men who would help form the nucleus of a great church in Ephesus. By using Paul to convey the gift of the Spirit, God affirmed Paul's apostolic authority and united the Ephesian church to the other churches as well as to the "mother" church in Jerusalem. When Peter and John laid hands on the believing Samaritans, it united them to the Jerusalem church and healed a breach between Jews and Samaritans that had existed for centuries.

What God did through Paul for these twelve men was not normative for the church today. How do we know? Because it was not repeated. The people who were converted in Ephesus under Paul's ministry all received the gift of the Holy Spirit *when they trusted the Saviour.* Paul makes this clear in Ephesians 1:13-14, and this is the pattern for us today.

In verse 6, we have the last instance of the gift of tongues in the Book of Acts. The believers spoke in tongues at Pentecost and praised God, and their listeners recognized these tongues as known languages (Acts 2:4-11) and not as some "heavenly speech." The Gentile believers in the house of Cornelius also spoke in tongues (10:44-46), and their experience was identical to that of the Jews in Acts 2 (see Acts 11:15). This was of historic significance since the Spirit was baptizing Jews (Acts 2) and Gentiles (Acts 10) into the body of Christ (see 1 Cor. 12:13).

Today, the gift of tongues is not an evidence of the baptism of the Spirit or the fullness of the Spirit. Paul asked, "Do all speak with tongues?" (1 Cor. 12:30) and the Greek construction demands "No" as an answer. When Paul wrote to his Ephesian friends about the filling of the Holy Spirit, he said nothing about tongues (Eph. 5:18ff). Nowhere in Scripture are we admonished to seek a baptism of the Holy Spirit, or to speak in tongues, but we are commanded to be filled with the Spirit. Read Paul's letter to the Ephesian church and note the many references to the Holy Spirit of God and His work in the believer.

3. Seven Men with Inadequate Power (19:11-20)

It is remarkable that Paul was able to witness in the synagogue for three months before he had to leave. No doubt the faithful ministry of Aquila and Priscilla played an important part in this success. However, hardness of heart set in (Heb. 3:7ff), so Paul left the synagogue and moved his ministry to a schoolroom, taking his disciples with him. He probably used the room during the "off hours" each day (11 A.M. to 4 P.M.), when many people would be resting. Paul ministered in this way for about two years and "all they who dwelt in Asia heard the word of the Lord Jesus, both Jews and Greeks" (v. 10).

What a victorious ministry! It appears that everybody knew what Paul was saying and doing! (See vv. 17 and 20.) Even Paul's enemies had to admit that the Word was spreading and people were being saved (v. 26). Two factors made this possible: the witness of the believers as they went from place to place, and the "special miracles" that God enabled Paul to perform in Ephesus (v. 11).

In Bible history, you will find three special periods of miracles: (1) the time of Moses; (2) the time of Elijah and Elisha; and (3) the time of Jesus and His apostles. Each period was less than 100 years. Depending on how some of these events are classified, the total number of miracles for all three periods is less than 100. Of course, not all the miracles were recorded. (See John 20:30-31.)

When our Lord performed miracles, He usually had at least three purposes in mind: (1) to show His compassion and meet human needs; (2) to teach a spiritual truth; and (3) to present His credentials as the Messiah. The apostles followed this same pattern in their miracles. In fact, the ability to do miracles was one of the proofs of apostolic authority (Heb. 2:1-4; 2 Cor. 12:12; Mark 16:20; Rom. 15:18-19). Miracles *of themselves* do not save lost sinners (John 2:23-25; Luke 16:27-31). Miracles must be tied to the message of the Word of God.

God enabled Paul to perform "special miracles" because Ephesus was a center for the occult (vv. 18-19), and Paul was demonstrating God's power right in Satan's territory. But keep in mind that wherever God's people minister the truth, Satan sends a counterfeit to oppose the work. Jesus taught this truth in His Parable of the Tares (Matt. 13:24-30, 36-43); Peter experienced it in Samaria (Acts 8:9ff); and Paul experienced it at Paphos (13:4-12). Satan imitates whatever God's people are doing, because he knows that the unsaved world cannot tell the difference (2 Cor. 11:13-15).

It was not unusual for Jewish priests to seek to cast out demons (Luke 11:19), but it was unusual for them to use the name of Jesus Christ. Since these men had no personal relationship with the Saviour, they had to invoke the name of Paul as well; but their scheme did not work. The demon said, "Jesus I recognize, and Paul I am acquainted with; but who are you?" (literal translation) The demonized man then attacked the seven priests and drove them from the house.

Had this exorcism succeeded, it would have discredited the name of Jesus Christ and the ministry of the church in Ephesus. (Paul faced a similar situation in Philippi. See 16:16ff.)

However, God used the scheme to defeat Satan and to bring conviction to the believers who were still involved in magical arts. Instead of disgracing the name of Jesus, the event magnified His name and caused the Word of God to spread even more rapidly.

The tense of the verbs in verse 18 indicates that the people "kept coming . . . kept confessing . . . kept showing." These believers apparently had not made a clean break with sin and were still practicing their magic, but the Lord had dealt with them. The total value of the magical books and spells that they burned was equivalent to the total salaries of 150 men working for a whole year! These people did not count the cost but repented and turned from their sins.

4. A Mob of Indignant Citizens (19:21-41)

In verse 21, we have the first mention of Paul's plan to go to Rome. The fulfilling of this plan will be described in the last third of the Book of Acts. Paul would soon write to the saints in Rome and express this desire to them (Rom. 1:13-15; 15:22-29). But first he had to visit the churches in Macedonia and Achaia in order to complete the "love offering" that he was taking for the poor saints in Jerusalem (1 Cor. 16:3-7; Rom. 15:25-33; Acts 24:17). While he remained in Ephesus (1 Cor. 16:8-9), he sent Timothy to help him finish the job (1 Cor. 4:17; 16:10-11).

It was at this point that Satan attacked again, not as the deceiver (2 Cor. 11:3-4), but as the destroyer (1 Peter 5:8), and the murderer (John 8:44). Satan incited the guild of silversmiths to stage a public protest against Paul and the Gospel. Paul may have been referring to this riot when he wrote, "I have fought with beasts at Ephesus" (1 Cor. 15:32). The enemy had been repeatedly defeated throughout Paul's three years of ministry in Ephesus. It would have been a master stroke on Satan's part to climax that ministry with a citywide attack that could result in Paul's arrest, or even his death.

Wherever the Gospel is preached in power, it will be opposed by people who make money from superstition and sin. Paul did not arouse the opposition of the silversmiths by picketing the temple of Diana or staging anti-idolatry rallies. All he did was teach the truth daily and send out his converts to witness to the lost people in the city. As more and more people got converted, fewer and fewer customers were available.

"For the love of money is a root of all kinds of evil" (1 Tim. 6:10, NKJV). Demetrius and his silversmiths were promoting idolatry and immorality in order to make a living, while Paul was declaring the true God and pointing people to cleansing and purity through the free grace of God. The silversmiths were really more concerned about their jobs and their income than they were about Diana and her temple, but they were wise enough not to make this known.

Benjamin Franklin said that a mob was "a monster with heads enough, but no brains." How sad it is when people permit themselves to be led by a few selfish leaders who know the art of manipulation. Demetrius made use of the two things the Ephesians loved the most: the honor of their city and the greatness of their goddess and her temple. Without the help of radio, TV, or newspaper, he got his propaganda machine going and soon had the whole city in an uproar.

Max Lerner wrote in *The Unfinished Country*, "Every mob, in its ignorance and blindness and bewilderment, is a League of Frightened Men that seeks reassurance in collective action." It was a "religious mob" that shouted "Crucify Him! Crucify Him!" to Pilate, and eventually got its way. Had this Ephesian mob succeeded in its plans, Paul would have been arrested and executed before the law could have stepped in to protect him.

The confused crowd, some 25,000 shouting people, finally

filled up the amphitheater; most of them did not know what was happening or why they were there. Since the mob could not find Paul, they seized two of his helpers, Gaius (*not* the Gaius of 20:4, Rom. 16:23, and 1 Cor. 1:14) and Aristarchus (20:4). Paul wanted to enter the theater—what an opportunity for preaching the Gospel!—but the believers and some of the city leaders wisely counseled him to stay away (vv. 30-31).

Before long, race prejudice entered the picture, when a Jew named Alexander tried to address the crowd (vv. 33-34). No doubt he wanted to explain to them that the Jews living in Ephesus did not endorse Paul's message or ministry, and, therefore, must not be made scapegoats just to satisfy the crowd. But his very presence only aroused the mob even more, and they shouted for two more hours, "Great is Diana of the Ephesians!" The crowd knew that the Jews did not approve of idols and would not honor Diana. The only thing that protected the Jews was the Roman law that gave them freedom of religion.

It was the city clerk who finally got matters under control, and he did it primarily for political reasons. Ephesus was permitted by Rome to exist as a "free city" with its own elected assembly, but the Romans would have rejoiced to find an excuse for removing these privileges (v. 40). The same tactics that the silversmiths used to arouse the mob, the clerk used to quiet and reassure them—the greatness of their city and of their goddess.

Luke records the official statement that the believers were innocent of any crime, either public (v. 37) or private (v. 38). Paul had this same kind of "official approval" in Philippi (16:35-40) and in Corinth (18:12-17); and he would receive it again after his arrest in Jerusalem. Throughout the Book of Acts, Luke makes it clear that the persecution of the Christian church was incited by the unbelieving Jews and not by the Romans. If anything, Paul used his Roman citizenship to protect himself, his friends, and the local assemblies.

The crowd was dismissed, and no doubt the people went home congratulating themselves that they had succeeded in defending their great city and their famous goddess. It is doubtful that many of them questioned the truthfulness of their religion or determined to investigate what Paul had been preaching for three years. It is much easier to believe a lie and follow the crowd.

But Ephesus is gone, and so is the worldwide worship of Diana of the Ephesians. The city and the temple are gone, and the silversmiths' guild is gone. Ephesus is a place visited primarily by archeologists and people on Holy Land tours. Yet the Gospel of God's grace and the church of Jesus Christ are still here! We have four inspired letters that were sent to the saints in Ephesus—Ephesians, 1 and 2 Timothy, and Revelation 2:1-7. The name of Paul is honored, but the name of Demetrius is forgotten. (Were it not for Paul, we would not have met Demetrius in the first place!)

The church ministers by persuasion, not propaganda. We share God's truth, not man's religious lies. Our motive is love, not anger, and the glory of God, not the praise of men. This is why the church goes on, and we must keep it so.

7

A Minister's Farewell

Acts 20

In the final third of the Book of Acts, Dr. Luke records Paul's journey to Jerusalem, his arrest there, and his voyage to Rome. The Gospel of Luke follows a similar pattern as Luke describes Christ's journey to Jerusalem to die (9:53; 13:33; 18:31; 19:11, 28). Much as Jesus set His face "like a flint" to do the Father's will (Luke 9:51; Isa. 50:7), so Paul determined to finish his course with joy, no matter what the cost might be (20:24).

This chapter describes three "farewell events" as Paul closed his ministry in Macedonia, Achaia, and Asia.

1. A Farewell Journey (20:1-5)

"I do not expect to visit this country again!" D.L. Moody spoke those words in 1867 when he made his first trip to England. He was so seasick during the voyage that he decided he would never sail again, but he made five more visits to England, seasickness notwithstanding.

Paul was ready for another journey. He wanted to make at least one more visit to the churches the Lord had helped him to found, because Paul was a man with a concerned heart. "The care of all the churches" was his greatest joy as well as his heaviest burden (2 Cor. 11:23-28).

After the riot, Paul left Ephesus and headed toward Macedonia and Achaia (see 19:21). He expected to meet Titus at Troas and get a report on the problems in Corinth, but Titus did not come (2 Cor. 2:12-13). The men finally met in Macedonia and Paul rejoiced over the good news Titus brought (2 Cor. 7:5-7). Paul had originally planned to make two visits to Corinth (2 Cor. 1:15-16), but instead he made one visit that lasted three months (1 Cor. 16:5-6; Acts 20:3). During that visit, he wrote his Epistle to the Romans.

Paul had two goals in mind as he visited the various churches. His main purpose was to encourage and strengthen the saints so that they might stand true to the Lord and be effective witnesses. His second purpose was to finish taking up the collection for the needy believers in Jerusalem (Rom. 15:25-27; 1 Cor. 16:1-9; 2 Cor. 8–9). The men who accompanied him (20:4) were representatives of the churches, appointed to travel with Paul and help handle the funds (2 Cor. 8:18-24).

Once again, Paul had to change his plans, this time because of a Jewish plot to kill him at sea. Instead of sailing from Corinth, he traveled overland through Achaia and Macedonia, sailing from Philippi to Troas, where his "team" agreed to rendezvous. As a person who dislikes travel and changes in plans, I admire Paul for his courage, stamina, and adaptability. In spite of the complications and delays in travel today, we have a much easier time than Paul did—and we complain! He kept going!

2. A Farewell Service (20:6-12)

Paul was not able to make it to Jerusalem for the annual Passover celebration, so now his goal was to arrive there at least by Pentecost (20:16). Note the pronoun change to "us" and "we," for Dr. Luke has now joined the party (see 16:17). He had probably been ministering at Philippi where he joined Paul for the last leg of the journey. Paul must have rejoiced to have Luke, Titus, and Timothy at his side again. The men remained at Troas a week so that they might fellowship with the believers there. Perhaps they were also waiting for the departure of the next ship.

Luke gives us a brief report of a local church service in Troas, and from it we learn something of how they met and worshiped the Lord. Consider the elements involved.

The Lord's Day. To begin with, they met on the first day of the week and not on the seventh day which was the Sabbath. (See also 1 Cor. 16:1-2.) The first day came to be called "the Lord's Day" because on it the Lord Jesus Christ arose from the dead (Rev. 1:10). We should also remember that the church was born on the first day of the week when the Spirit came at Pentecost. During the early years of the church, the believers did maintain some of the Jewish traditions, such as the hours of prayer (3:1). But as time went on, they moved away from the Mosaic calendar and developed their own pattern of worship as the Spirit taught them.

The Lord's people. The church met in the evening because Sunday was not a holiday during which people were free from daily employment. Some of the believers would no doubt be slaves, unable to come to the assembly until their work was done. The believers met in an upper room because they had no church buildings in which to gather. This room may have been in the private home of one of the believers. The assembly would have been a cosmopolitan group, but their social and national distinctions made no difference: they were "all one in Christ Jesus" (Gal. 3:28).

The Lord's Supper. The early church shared a "potluck" meal called the "love feast" (*agape*), after which they would observe the Lord's Supper (Acts 2:42; 1 Cor. 11:17-34). The "breaking of bread" in verse 7 refers to the Lord's Supper, whereas in verse 11 it describes a regular meal. By sharing and eating with one another, the church enjoyed fellowship and also gave witness of their oneness in Christ. Slaves would actually eat at the same table with their masters, something unheard of in that day.

It is likely that the church observed the Lord's Supper each Lord's Day when they met for fellowship and worship. In fact, some believers probably ended many of their regular meals at home by taking the bread and wine and remembering the Lord's death. While Scripture does not give us specific instructions in the matter ("as often," 1 Cor. 11:26), the example of the early church would encourage us to meet at the Lord's table often. However, the Communion must not become routine, causing us to fail to receive the blessings involved.

The Lord's message. The Word of God was always declared in the Christian assemblies, and this included the public reading of the Old Testament Scriptures (1 Tim. 4:13) as well as whatever apostolic letters had been received (Col. 4:16). It is sad to see how the Word is neglected in church services today. Knowing that this would probably be his last meeting with the saints at Troas, Paul preached a long sermon, after which he ate and conversed with the people until morning. It's doubtful that anybody complained. How we today wish we could have been there to hear the Apostle Paul preach!

The Word of God is important to the people of God, and the preaching and teaching of the Word must be emphasized. The church meets for edification as well as for celebration, and that edification comes through the Word. "Preach the Word!" is still God's admonition to spiritual leaders (2 Tim. 4:2). According to Dr. D. Martyn Lloyd-Jones, "the decadent periods and eras in the history of the church have always been those periods when preaching has declined" (*Preachers and Preaching*, Zondervan, p. 24).

The Lord's power. Whether it was the lateness of the hour or the stuffiness of the room (surely not the dullness of Paul's sermon!), Eutychus ("Fortunate") fell asleep and then fell out the window, and was killed by the fall. However, Paul raised him from the dead and left him and the church comforted. God's power was present to work for His people.

How old was Eutychus? The Greek word *neanias* in verse 9 means a man from twenty-four to forty years of age. The word *pais* in verse 12 means a young child or youth. Dr. Howard Marshall, an eminent Greek scholar, says he was a "young lad of eight to fourteen years. Since the word *pais* can mean "a servant," Eutychus may have been a young man who was also a servant. He may have worked hard that day and was weary. No wonder he fell asleep during the lengthy sermon!

Let's not be too hard on Eutychus. At least he was there for the service, and he did try to keep awake. He sat near ventilation, and he must have tried to fight off the sleep that finally conquered him. The tense of the Greek verb indicates that he was gradually overcome, not suddenly.

Also, let's not be too hard on Paul. After all, he was preaching his farewell sermon to this assembly, and he had a great deal to tell them for their own good. Those sitting near should have been watching Eutychus; but, of course, they were engrossed in what Paul was saying. Paul did interrupt his sermon to rush downstairs to bring the young man back to life. His approach reminds us of Elijah (1 Kings 17:21-22) and Elisha (2 Kings 4:34-35).

Perhaps each of us should ask ourselves, "What really keeps me awake?" Christians who slumber during one hour in church somehow manage to stay awake during early-morning fishing trips, lengthy sporting events and concerts, or late-night TV specials. Also, we need to prepare ourselves physically for public worship to make sure we are at our best. "Remember," said Spurgeon, "if we go to sleep during the sermon and die, there are no apostles to restore us!"

3. A Farewell Message (20:13-38)

Paul chose to walk from Troas to Assos, a distance of about twenty miles. Why? For one thing, it enabled him to stay longer with the saints in Troas while he sent Luke and the party on ahead (v. 13). It would take the ship at least a day to sail from Troas to Assos, and Paul could probably walk it in ten hours or less. Also, Paul probably wanted time alone to commune with the Lord about his trip to Jerusalem. The apostle must have sensed already that difficult days lay ahead of him. He may also have been pondering the message he would give to the Ephesian elders. Finally, the exercise was certainly beneficial! Even inspired apostles need to care for their bodies. I personally would prefer walking to sailing!

There were fifty days between Passover (v. 6) and Pentecost (v. 16), and Paul's trip from Philippi to Troas had already consumed twelve of them (v. 6). It took another four days to get to Miletus, so Paul decided not to go to Ephesus lest he lose any more valuable time. Instead, he invited the leaders of the Ephesian church to travel about thirty miles and meet him at Miletus, where the ship was waiting to unload cargo and take on more. Paul was not one to waste time or to lose opportunities.

In the Book of Acts, Luke reports eight messages given by the Apostle Paul to various people: a Jewish synagogue congregation (13:14-43); Gentiles (14:14-18; 17:22-34); church leaders (20:17-38); a Jewish mob (22:1-21); the Jewish council (23:1-10); and various government officials (24:10-21; 26:1-32). His address to the Ephesian elders is unique in that it reveals Paul the pastor rather than Paul the evangelist or Paul the defender of the faith. The message enables us to get a glimpse of how Paul ministered in Ephesus for three years.

The word *elder* is *presbutos* in the Greek ("presbyter") and refers to a mature person who has been selected to serve in office (14:23). These same people are called "overseers" in verse 28, which is *episkopos* or bishop. They were chosen to "feed the church" (v. 28), which means "to shepherd." Paul called the local church "a flock, (vv. 28-29), so these men were also pastors. (The word *pastor* means "shepherd.") Thus in the New Testament churches, the three titles *elder, bishop,* and *pastor* were synonymous. The qualifications for this office are given in 1 Timothy 3:1-7 and Titus 1:5-9.

There were three parts to Paul's farewell message. First he reviewed the past (vv. 18-21); then he discussed the present (vv. 22-27); and finally, he spoke about the future (vv. 28-35). In the first part, he emphasized his faithfulness to the Lord and to the church as he ministered for three years in Ephesus. The second section reveals Paul's personal feelings in view of both the past and the future. In the third part, he warned them of the dangers that the churches faced.

A review of the past (vv. 18-21). Paul was not one to work into his ministry gradually like a diplomat feeling his way. "From the first day" he gave himself unsparingly to the work of the Lord in Ephesus, for Paul was an ambassador and not a diplomat.

The *motive* for Paul's ministry is found in the phrase "serving the Lord" (v. 19). He was not interested in making money (v. 33) or in enjoying an easy life (vv. 34-35), for he was the bondslave of Jesus Christ (v. 24; Rom. 1:1). Paul was careful to let people know that his motives for ministry were spiritual and not selfish (1 Thes. 2:1-13).

The *manner* of his ministry was exemplary (vv. 18-19). He lived a consistent life which anybody could inspect, for he had nothing to hide. He served in humility and not as a "religious celebrity" demanding that others serve him. But his humility was not a sign of weakness, for he had the courage to face trials and dangers without quitting. Paul was not ashamed to admit to his friends that there had also been times of tears. (See also vv. 31, 37, and Rom. 9:1-2; 2 Cor. 2:4; Phil. 3:18.)

The *message* of his ministry (vv. 20-21) was also widely known, because he announced it and taught it publicly (19:9) as well as in the various house churches of the fellowship. He told sinners to repent of their sins and believe in Jesus Christ. This message was "the Gospel of the grace of God" (v. 24), and it is the *only* message that can save the sinner (1 Cor. 15:1-8; Gal. 1:6-12).

Furthermore, Paul reminded them that, in his ministry, he had not held back anything that was profitable to them. He declared to them "all the counsel of God" (v. 27). His was a balanced message that included the doctrines and duties, as well as the privileges and responsibilities, that belonged to the Christian life. In his preaching, he neither compromised nor went to extremes, but kept things in balance. Paul also kept his outlook congregation balanced, witnessing both to Jews and to Gentiles.

A testimony of the present (vv. 22-27). The phrase "And now, behold" shifts the emphasis from the past to the present as Paul opens his heart and tells his friends just how he feels. He did not hide from them the fact that he was bound in his spirit (19:21) to go to Jerusalem, even though he knew that danger and possible death awaited him there. The Holy Spirit had witnessed this message to him in city after city. A lesser man would have found some way to escape, but not Paul. He was too gripped by his calling and his devotion to Jesus Christ to look for some safe and easy way out. In his testimony, Paul used six graphic pictures of his ministry to explain why he would not quit but would go to Jerusalem to die for Jesus Christ if necessary. Paul could say "None of these things move me!" because he knew what he was as a minister of Jesus Christ.

Paul saw himself as *an accountant* (v. 24) who had examined his assets and liabilities and decided to put Jesus Christ ahead of everything else. He had faced this kind of reckoning early in his ministry and had willingly made the spiritual the number one priority in his life (Phil. 3:1-11).

He also saw himself as a *runner* who wanted to finish his course in joyful victory (Phil. 3:12-14; 2 Tim. 4:8). The three phrases "my life, my course, the ministry" are the key. Paul realized that his life was God's gift to him, and that God had a special plan for his life that would be fulfilled in his ministry. Paul was devoted to a great Person ("serving the Lord") and motivated by a great purpose, the building of the church.

Paul's third picture is that of the *steward*, for his ministry was something that he had "received of the Lord." The steward owns little or nothing, but he possesses all things. His sole purpose is to serve his master and please him. "Moreover it is required in stewards that one be found faithful" (1 Cor. 4:2, NKJV). The steward must one day give an account of his ministry, and Paul was ready for that day.

The next picture is that of the *witness*, "testifying of the Gospel of the grace of God" (v. 24, and note v. 21). The word means "to solemnly give witness," and it reminds us of the seriousness of the message and of the ministry. As we share the Gospel with others, it is a matter of life or death (2 Cor. 2:15-16). Paul was a faithful witness both in the life that he lived (v. 18) and the message that he preached.

Picture number five is the *herald* (v. 25). The word *preaching* means "to declare a message as the herald of the king." The witness tells what has happened to him, but the herald tells what the king tells him to declare. He is a man commissioned and sent with a message, and he must not change that message in any way. And since he is sent by the king, the people who listen had better be careful how they treat both the messenger and the message.

The final picture, and perhaps the most dramatic, is that of the *watchman* (v. 26). As in 18:6, this is a reference to the "watchman on the walls" in Ezekiel 3:17-21 and 33:1-9. What a serious calling it was to be a watchman! He had to stay awake and alert, ready to sound the alarm if he saw danger approaching. He had to be faithful, not fearful, because the safety of many people rested with him. Paul had been a faithful watchman (v. 31), for he had declared to sinners and saints all the counsel of God. Unfortunately, we have today many unfaithful watchmen who think only of themselves (Isa. 56:10-13).

A group of servicemen asked their new chaplain if he believed in a real hell for lost sinners, and he smiled and told them that he did not. "Then you are wasting your time," the men replied. "If there is no hell, we don't need you; and if there is a hell, you are leading us astray. Either way, we're better off without you!"

A warning about the future (vv. 28-35). Paul brought his farewell message to a close by warning the leaders of the dangers they had to recognize and deal with if they were to protect and lead the church. Never underestimate the great importance of the church. The church is important to God the Father because His name is upon it—"the church of God." It is important to the Son because He shed His blood for it; and it is important to the Holy Spirit because He is calling and equipping people to minister to the church. It is a serious thing to be a spiritual leader in the church of the living God.

To begin with, there are dangers *around us*, "wolves" that want to ravage the flock (v. 29). Paul was referring to false teachers, the counterfeits who exploit the church for personal gain (Matt. 7:15-23; 10:16; Luke 10:3; 2 Peter 2:1-3). How important it is that believers know the Word of God and be able to detect and defeat these religious racketeers.

But there are also dangers *among us* (v. 30), because of people within the church who are ambitious for position and power. Church history, ancient and modern, is filled with accounts of people like Diotrephes who love to have the pre-eminence (3 John 9-11). It is shocking to realize that more than one false prophet got his or her start within the Christian church family! Read 1 John 2:18-19 and take heed.

There are also dangers *within us* (vv. 31-35), and this seems to be where Paul put the greatest emphasis. "Take heed, therefore, unto yourselves" (v. 28). He names five sins that are especially destructive to the life and ministry of spiritual leaders in the church.

The first is *carelessness* (v. 31), failing to stay alert and forgetting the price that others have paid so that we might have God's truth. "Watch and remember!" are words we had better heed. It is so easy for us today to forget the toil and tears of those who labored before us (Heb. 13:7). Paul's warning and weeping should be constant reminders to us to take our spiritual responsibilities seriously.

The second sin is *shallowness* (v. 32). We cannot build the church unless God is building our lives daily. There is a balance here between prayer ("I commend you to God") and the Word of God ("the word of His grace"), because these two must always work together (Acts 6:4; 1 Sam. 12:23; John 15:7). The Word of God alone is able to edify and enrich us, and the spiritual leader must spend time daily in the Word of God and prayer.

Covetousness is the third sin we must avoid (v. 33). It means a consuming and controlling desire for what others have and for more of what we ourselves already have. "Thou shalt not covet" is the last of the Ten Commandments, but if we do covet, we will end up breaking all the other nine! Those who covet will steal, lie, and murder to get what they want, and even dishonor their own parents. Covetousness is idolatry (Eph. 5:5; Col. 3:5). In the qualifications for an elder, it is expressly stated that he must not be guilty of the sin of covetousness (1 Tim. 3:3).

Paul also mentioned *laziness* (v. 34). Paul earned his own way as a tentmaker, even though he could have used his apostolic authority to demand support and thereby have an easier life. It is not wrong for Christian workers to receive salaries, for "the laborer is worthy of his hire" (Luke 10:7; 1 Tim. 5:18). But they should be certain that they are really *earning* those salaries! (Read Proverbs 24:30-34.)

Finally, Paul warned about *selfishness* (v. 35). True ministry means giving, not getting; it means following the example of the Lord Jesus Christ. Dr. Earl V. Pierce used to call this "the supreme beatitude" because, unlike the other beatitudes, it tells us how to be *more* blessed! These words of Jesus are not found anywhere in the Gospels, but they were a part of the oral tradition, and Paul memorized them.

This beatitude does not suggest that people who receive are "less blessed" than people who give. (The beggar in Acts 3 would argue about that!) It could be paraphrased, "It's better to share with others than to keep what you have and collect more." In other words, the blessing does not come in accumulating wealth, but in sharing it. After all, Jesus became poor that we might become rich (2 Cor. 8:9). One of the best commentaries on this statement is Luke 12:16-31.

Paul closed this memorable occasion by kneeling down and praying for his friends, and then they all wept together. It is a difficult thing to say good-bye, especially when you know you will not see your friends again in this life. But we have the blessed assurance that we will one day see our Christian friends and loved ones in heaven, when Jesus Christ returns (1 Thes. 4:13-18).

Meanwhile, there is a job to be done—so, let's do it!

8

The Misunderstood Missionary

Acts 21:1–22:29

"Is it so bad, then, to be misunderstood?" asked Ralph Waldo Emerson. "Pythagoras was misunderstood, and Socrates, and Jesus, and Luther, and Copernicus, and Galileo, and Newton. . . . To be great is to be misunderstood."

Emerson might have added that the Apostle Paul was misunderstood, by friends and foes alike. Three of these misunderstandings—and their consequences—are recorded in these chapters.

1. Paul's Friends Misunderstood His Plans (21:1-17)

Paul had to tear himself away from the Ephesian elders, so great was his love for them. He and his party sailed from Miletus to Cos, then to Rhodes, and then to Patera, a total of three days' journey. But Paul was uncomfortable with a "local coastal" ship that stopped at every port; so when he found a boat going directly to Phoenicia, he and his friends boarded it. It would be a voyage of about 400 miles.

Tyre (vv. 3-6). This would have been Paul's first contact with the believers in Tyre, although it is likely that his persecution of the Jerusalem believers helped to get this church started (11:19). The men had to seek out the believers, so it must not have been a large assembly; and apparently there was no synagogue in the town. They stayed a week with the saints while their ship unloaded its cargo and took on new cargo.

Paul had devoted a good part of his third missionary journey to taking up a love gift for the Jews in Judea. It was a practical way for the Gentiles to show their oneness with their Jewish brothers and sisters, and to repay them for sharing the Gospel with the Gentiles (Rom. 15:25-27). There was in the church a constant threat of division, for the Jewish extremists (the Judaizers) wanted the Gentiles to live like Jews and follow the Law of Moses (Acts 15:1ff). Wherever Paul ministered, these extremists tried to hinder his work and steal his converts. Paul hoped that his visit to Jerusalem with the offering would help to strengthen the fellowship between Jews and Gentiles.

Now, Paul began to get messages from his friends that his visit to Jerusalem would be difficult and dangerous. Of course, he had already suspected this, knowing how the false teachers operated (Rom. 15:30-31); but these messages were very personal and powerful. In Tyre, the believers "kept on saying to him" (literal Greek) that he should not set foot in Jerusalem.

After a week in Tyre, Paul and his party departed. It is touching to see how the believers had come to love Paul, though they had known him only a week. The first stop was Ptolemais, where they visited the believers for a day; and then they sailed to Caesarea, their final destination.

Caesarea (vv. 7-14). The men stayed with Philip, one of the original deacons (6:1-6) who also served as an evangelist (8:5ff). It was now some twenty years since he had come to Caesarea and made it his headquarters (8:40). Since Philip had been an associate of Stephen, and Paul had taken part in Stephen's death, this must have been an interesting meeting.

While Paul rested in Caesarea, the Prophet Agabus came to give him a second warning message from the Lord. Some fifteen years before, Paul and Agabus had worked together in a famine relief program for Judea (11:27-30), so they were not strangers. Agabus delivered his message in a dramatic way as he bound his own hands and feet with Paul's girdle and told the apostle that he would be bound in Jerusalem.

As did the saints in Tyre, so the believers in Caesarea begged Paul not to go to Jerusalem. Surely the men chosen by the churches could deliver the love offering to James and the Jerusalem elders, and it would not be necessary for Paul to go personally. But Paul silenced them and told them that he was prepared ("ready") not only to be bound, but also to die if necessary for the name of the Lord Jesus Christ.

Now we must pause to consider whether Paul was right or wrong in making that trip to Jerusalem. If it seems improper, or even blasphemous, so to examine the actions of an apostle, keep in mind that he was a human being like anyone else. His epistles were inspired, but this does not necessarily mean that everything he did was perfect. Whether he was right or wrong, we can certainly learn from his experience.

On the *con* side, these repeated messages do sound like warnings to Paul to stay out of Jerusalem. For that matter, over twenty years before, the Lord had commanded Paul to get out of Jerusalem because the Jews would not receive his testimony (22:18). Paul had already written to the Romans about the dangers in Judea (15:30-31), and he had shared these same feelings with the Ephesian elders (20:22-23); so he was fully aware of the problems involved.

On the *pro* side, the prophetic utterances can be taken as warnings ("Get ready!") rather than as prohibitions ("You must not go!"). The statement in 21:4 does not use the Greek negative *ou*, which means absolute prohibition, but *me*, used "where one *thinks* a thing is not" (*Manual Greek Lexicon of the New Testament*, by G. Abbott-Smith, p. 289). Agabus did not forbid Paul to go to Jerusalem; he only told him what to expect if he did go. As for the Lord's command in 22:18, it applied to that particular time and need not be interpreted as a prohibition governing the rest of Paul's life. While it is true that Paul avoided Jerusalem, it is also true that he returned there on other occasions: with famine relief (11:27-30); to attend the Jerusalem conference (15:1ff); and after his second missionary journey (18:22—"going up to greet the church" refers to Jerusalem).

In view of Paul's statement in Acts 23:1, and the Lord's encouraging words in 23:11, it is difficult to believe that the apostle deliberately disobeyed the revealed will of God. God's prophecy to Ananias (9:15) certainly came true in the months that followed as Paul had opportunity to witness for Christ.

Instead of accusing Paul of compromise, we ought to applaud him for his courage. Why? Because in going to Jerusalem, he took his life in his hands in order to try to solve the most pressing problem in the church: the growing division between the "far right" legalistic Jews and the believing Gentiles. Ever since the Jerusalem conference (Acts 15), trouble had been brewing; and the legalists had been following Paul and seeking to capture his converts. It was a serious situation, and Paul knew that he was a part of the answer as well as a part of the problem. But he could not solve the problem by remote control through representatives; he had to go to Jerusalem personally.

Jerusalem (vv. 15-17). A company of believers left Caesarea and traveled with Paul to Jerusalem, probably to celebrate the feast. It was a journey of sixty-five miles that took at least three days by foot—two days if they had animals. What fellowship they must have enjoyed as they recounted what God had done in and through them! What a great encouragement it was for Paul to have these friends at his side as he faced the challenge of Jerusalem.

The city would be crowded with pilgrims, but Paul and his party planned to live with Mnason, "an early disciple," who lived in Jerusalem and had been visiting Caesarea. Was he perhaps converted under Peter's preaching at Pentecost? Or did his fellow Cypriot Barnabas win him to Christ? (4:36) We are not told; but we do know that Mnason was a man given to hospitality, and his ministry helped Paul at a strategic time in the apostle's ministry.

We could wish that Dr. Luke had told us more about that first meeting with the church leaders in Jerusalem. James and the other leaders did receive them gladly, but how did they respond to the gift from the Gentiles? Nothing is said about it. Were some of them perhaps a bit suspicious? A few years later, the Roman writer Martial would say, "Gifts are like hooks!" and perhaps some of the Jerusalem elders felt that way about this gift. Certainly the legalistic wing of the church would question anything that Paul said or did.

2. The Jerusalem Church Misunderstood His Message (21:18-26)

Apparently that first meeting was devoted primarily to fellowship and personal matters, because the second meeting was given over to Paul's personal report of his ministry to the Gentiles. The Jerusalem leaders had agreed years before that Paul should minister to the Gentiles (Gal. 2:7-10), and the elders rejoiced at what they heard. The phrase "declared particularly" means "reported in detail, item by item." Paul gave a full and accurate account, not of what he had done, but of what the Lord had done through his ministry (see 1 Cor. 15:10).

You get the impression that the legalists had been working

behind the scenes. No sooner had Paul finished his report than the elders brought up the rumors that were then being circulated about Paul among the Jewish Christians. It has well been said that, though a rumor doesn't have a leg to stand on, it travels mighty fast!

What were his enemies saying about Paul? Almost the same things they said about Jesus and Stephen: he was teaching the Jews to forsake the laws and customs given by Moses and the fathers. They were not worried about what Paul taught the Gentile believers, because the relationship of the Gentiles to the Law had been settled at the Jerusalem conference (Acts 15). In fact, the elders carefully rehearsed the matter (v. 25), probably for the sake of Paul's Gentile companions. The leaders were especially concerned that Paul's presence in the city not cause division or disruption among the "thousands of Jews . . . zealous of the Law" (v. 20).

But, why were so many believing Jews still clinging to the Law of Moses? Had they not read Romans and Galatians? Probably not, and even if they had, old customs are difficult to change. In fact, one day God would have to send a special letter to the Jews, the Epistle to the Hebrews, to explain the relationship between the Old and New Covenants. As Dr. Donald Grey Barnhouse used to say, "The Book of Hebrews was written to the Hebrews to tell them to stop being Hebrews!" It was not until the city and the temple were destroyed in A.D. 70 that traditional Jewish worship ceased.

Paul did warn the Gentiles not to get involved in the old Jewish religion (Gal. 4:1-11); but he nowhere told the Jews that it was wrong for them to practice their customs, *so long as they did not trust in ceremony or make their customs a test of fellowship* (Rom. 14:1–15:7). There was freedom to observe special days and diets, and believers were not to judge or condemn one another. The same grace that gave the Gentiles freedom to abstain also gave the Jews freedom to observe. All God asked was that they receive one another and not create problems or divisions.

It seems incredible that Paul's enemies would accuse him of these things, for all the evidence was against them. Paul had Timothy circumcised before taking him along on that second missionary journey (16:1-3). Paul had taken a Jewish vow while in Corinth (18:18), and it was his custom not to offend the Jews in any way by deliberately violating their customs or the Law of Moses (1 Cor. 9:19-23). However, rumors are not usually based on fact, but thrive on half-truths, prejudices, and outright lies.

The leaders suggested that Paul demonstrate publicly his reverence for the Jewish Law. All they asked was that he identify himself with four men under a Nazirite vow (Num. 6), pay for their sacrifices, and be with them in the temple for their time of purification. He agreed to do it. If it had been a matter involving somebody's personal salvation, you can be sure that Paul would never have cooperated; for that would have compromised his message of salvation by grace, through faith. But this was a matter of personal conviction on the part of Jewish believers who were given the freedom to accept or reject the customs.

Paul reported to the priest the next day and shared in the purification ceremony, but he himself did not take any vows. He and the men had to wait seven days and then offer the prescribed sacrifices. The whole plan appeared to be safe and wise, but it did not work. Instead of bringing peace, it caused an uproar; and Paul ended up a prisoner.

3. The Jews Misunderstood Paul's Ministry (21:27–22:29)

In the temple, separating the Court of the Gentiles from the other courts, stood a wall beyond which no Gentile was allowed to go. (Note Eph. 2:14.) On the wall was this solemn inscription: "No foreigner may enter within the barricade which surrounds the sanctuary and enclosure. Anyone who is caught so doing will have himself to blame for his ensuing death." The Romans had granted the Jewish religious leaders authority to deal with anybody who broke this law, and this included the right of execution. This law plays an important role in what happened to Paul a week after he and the four Nazirites began their purification ceremonies.

Some Jews from Asia saw Paul in the temple and jumped to the conclusion that he had polluted their sacred building by bringing Gentiles past the barricade. It is likely that these Jews came from Ephesus, because they recognized Paul's friend Trophimus, who came from Ephesus. With their emotions running at full speed, and their brains in neutral, these men argued: (1) wherever Paul went, his Gentile friends went; (2) Paul was seen in the temple; therefore, his friends had been in the temple too! Such is the logic of prejudice.

They seized Paul and would have killed him had the Roman guards not intervened in the nick of time. (At least 1,000 soldiers were stationed in the Antonia Fortress at the northwest corner of the temple area.) The temple crowd was in an uproar, completely ignorant of what was going on. The scene reminds you of the riot in Ephesus. Compare verse 30 with 19:29 and verse 34 with 19:32. It required the chief captain (Claudius Lysias, 23:26), 2 centurions, and perhaps 200 soldiers to get the mob under control and to rescue Paul. The captain actually thought Paul was an Egyptian rebel who was wanted by the Romans for inciting a revolt (v. 38). This explains why he had Paul bound with two chains (see v. 11).

When Claudius interrogated the people, they could not explain what caused the riot because they did not really know. The original troublemakers must have escaped during the great excitement, knowing that they could not actually substantiate their charges. Since Claudius could get no help from the people in the temple, he decided to interrogate Paul; so his soldiers carried Paul from the Court of the Gentiles up the stairs into the barracks. As Paul was borne away, the crowd shouted angrily, "Away with him!" This again reminds us of our Lord's arrest and trial (Luke 23:18, 21; John 19:15).

At this point, Paul decided it was time to speak up; and the captain was amazed that his dangerous prisoner could speak Greek. When Paul asked for permission to address the Jews, Claudius consented, hoping that perhaps he would get enough information for an official report. He never did (see 23:23-30). Paul spoke to the Jews in their native Aramaic, and this helped quiet them down. He was never able to finish his speech, but he did get to explain three important aspects of his life and ministry.

His early conduct (vv. 3-5). Paul had been a leading rabbi in his day (Gal. 1:13-14), so he was certainly known to some of the people in the crowd. Note how Paul piled up his Jewish credentials: he was a Jew, a native of Tarsus, brought up in Jerusalem, trained by Gamaliel, a follower of the Law, a zealous persecutor of the church, and a representative of the Sanhedrin. How could his countrymen not respectfully listen to a man with that kind of record!

Instead of accusing them of participating in a riot, he commended them for being "zealous toward God." (He had used a similar approach with the Athenians; 17:22.) He admitted that he too had been guilty of having people arrested and bound, and even killed. The Christian faith was known as "the way" (9:2; 19:9, 23; 24:14, 22), probably a reference to our Lord's statement, "I am the way" (John 14:6).

His wonderful conversion (vv. 6-16). Luke recorded Paul's conversion experience in chapter 9, and Paul will repeat the account later for Felix and Agrippa (26:1-32). It is difficult to imagine a comparable crowd today quietly listening to that kind of a testimony. However, people in that day expected miraculous things to happen and were no doubt fascinated by Paul's story (see 23:9). Also, Paul was on official Sanhedrin business when these events took place, which at least gave it some aura of authority.

In his testimony, Paul affirmed that Jesus of Nazareth was alive. Paul saw His glory and heard His voice. The people listening in the temple courts knew the official Jewish position that Jesus of Nazareth was an imposter who had been crucified and His body stolen from the tomb by His disciples who then started the rumor that Jesus had been raised from the dead. Of course, Paul himself had believed this story when he was persecuting the church.

The men with Paul saw the bright light, but were not blinded as he was; and they heard a sound, but could not understand what was being spoken (9:7). Imagine Paul's amazement to discover that Jesus was alive! Instantly, he had to change his whole way of thinking (repentance) and let the risen Lord have control.

Note Paul's wisdom as he identified himself with Ananias, a devout Jew who kept the Law and who called him "brother." Note also that Ananias attributed Paul's great experience to "the God of our fathers." In quoting Ananias, Paul gave reason for his listeners to accept his salvation experience and his call to service. Paul had seen "the Just [Righteous] One," which was a title for Messiah (see 3:14 and 7:52). Paul was now commissioned by God to take His message to "all men." This would include the Gentiles, but Paul did not say so until later.

Verse 16 in the *King James Version* seems to suggest that baptism is required for the washing away of our sins, but such is not the case. In his *Expanded Translation of the New Testament*, Greek scholar Kenneth Wuest puts it, "Having arisen, be baptized and wash away your sins, having previously called upon His Name." We are saved by calling on the

Lord by faith (2:21; 9:14), and we give evidence of that faith by being baptized. According to 9:17, Paul was filled with the Spirit *before* he was baptized; and this would indicate that he was already born again. It is the "calling," not the baptizing, that effects the cleansing.

Certainly many of Paul's listeners knew about the new "Christian sect" that had sprung up, the baptisms that had taken place, the stoning of Stephen, and the miracles that these "people of the way" had wrought. Paul was not speaking to ignorant people, because these things had not been "done in a corner" (26:26).

His special calling (vv. 17-21). After his conversion, Paul had ministered in Damascus and then had gone to Arabia, perhaps to evangelize and to meditate on God's Word (9:19-25; Gal. 1:16-17). When Paul did return to Jerusalem, the church leaders did not accept him until Barnabas interceded and got him in (9:26-29). Note how Paul again emphasized the Jewish elements in his experience, for the Jews would be impressed with a man who prayed in the temple and had a vision from God.

The Lord told Paul to leave Jerusalem quickly, because the people would not receive his witness. By obeying this command, Paul saved his life, because the Hellenistic Jews had plotted to kill him (9:29-30). But first, Paul debated with the Lord! He wanted to show the Jews that he was a new person and tell them that Jesus was the Messiah, and He was alive. If Paul won some of them to the Lord, it would perhaps help to compensate for all the damage he had done, especially in the killing of Stephen.

The Lord's command was, "Depart, for I will send you far from here to the Gentiles!" (v. 21, NKJV) Paul was about to explain why he was involved with the Gentiles, but the Jews in the temple courts would not permit him to go on. No devout Jew would have anything to do with the Gentiles! Had

Paul not uttered that one word, he might have later been released; *and perhaps he knew this.* However, he had to be faithful in his witness, no matter what it cost him. Paul would rather be a prisoner than give up his burden for lost souls and for missions! We could use more Christians like that today.

When Claudius saw that the riot was starting again, he took Paul into the barracks for "examination by torture." The apostle had already mentioned that he was born in Tarsus, but he had not told them that his citizenship was Roman. It was unlawful for a Roman citizen to be scourged. We do not know how people proved their citizenship in those days; perhaps they carried the first-century equivalent of an ID card.

Claudius must have been shocked that this little Jewish troublemaker who spoke Aramaic and Greek was actually a Roman citizen. "With great sum I obtained this freedom," Claudius boasted, indicating that he had gotten his citizenship by bribing the Roman officials, for it could not be actually purchased. But Paul was ahead of the Roman captain, for he had been born into freedom and Roman citizenship, thanks to his father. How Paul's father obtained his freedom, we do not know. We do know that Paul knew how to make use of his Roman citizenship for the cause of Christ.

The soldiers had made two mistakes, and they were quick to undo them: they had bound Paul and had planned to scourge him. No doubt Claudius and his men were especially kind to Paul now that they knew he was a Roman citizen. God was using the great power of the Empire to protect His servant and eventually get him to Rome.

Paul's entire time in Jerusalem was one filled with serious misunderstandings, but he pressed on. Perhaps at this point some of his friends were saying, "We told him so! We warned him!" For Paul and his associates, it may have looked like the end of the road, but God had other plans for them. Paul would witness again and again, and to people he could never have met had he not been a Roman prisoner. God's mission-ary did get to Rome—and the Romans paid the bill!

That's what happens when God's people are willing to be daring!

9

Paul the Prisoner

Acts 22:30–23:35

I was once called to be a character witness in a child custody case involving a man who had served time in prison. This was a new experience for me, and I was completely unprepared for the first question the attorney asked me: "Reverend, do you think that a man who has been a prisoner is fit to raise a child?"

"That depends on the man," I replied bravely. "Some of the greatest men in history have been prisoners—John the Baptist, John Bunyan, and even the Apostle Paul."

"Simply answer yes or no!" said the judge curtly, and that was the end of my sermon.

"Paul the prisoner" (v. 18) was the name the Roman soldiers used for the apostle, a designation he himself often used (Eph. 3:1; 4:1; 2 Tim. 1:8; Phile. 1, 9). Paul was under "military custody," which meant he was bound to a Roman soldier who was responsible for him. Prisoners under "public custody" were put in the common jail, a horrible place for any human being to suffer (Acts 16:19-24).

Paul's friends could visit him and help meet his personal

needs. It is sad that we don't read, "And prayer was made fervently by the church for Paul" (see 12:5). There is no record that the Jerusalem church took any steps to assist him, either in Jerusalem or during his two years in Caesarea.

This is an exciting chapter, and in it we read of three confrontations that Paul experienced.

1. Paul and the Jewish Council (22:30–23:10)

Having discovered that Paul was a Roman citizen, the Roman captain now had two serious problems to solve. First, he needed to let the prisoner know what the official charges were against him, since that was Paul's right as a Roman citizen. Second, he also needed to have some official charges for his own records and to share with his superiors. He was sure that Paul had done something notorious, otherwise why would so many people want to do away with him? Yet nobody seemed to know what Paul's crimes were. What a plight for a Roman official to be in!

The logical thing was to let Paul's own people try him, so the captain arranged for a special meeting of the Jewish council (Sanhedrin). This group was composed of 70 (or 71) of the leading Jewish teachers, with the high priest presiding. It was their responsibility to interpret and apply the sacred Jewish Law to the affairs of the nation, and to try those who violated that Law. The Romans gave the council permission to impose capital punishment where the offense deserved it.

The captain and his guard (v. 10) brought Paul into the council chamber and stepped aside to watch the proceedings. Knowing how the Jews in the temple had treated Paul, Claudius remained there on guard lest his prisoner be taken from him and killed. No Roman soldier could afford to lose a prisoner, for that might mean the forfeiting of his own life. The loss of a prisoner against whom the charges were nebulous would be especially embarrassing for any Roman officer.

As Paul faced the council and examined it carefully, he decided to start with a personal approach. "Men and brethren" immediately identified him as a Jew and no doubt helped win the attention of his countrymen.

The Greek word translated "lived" means "to live as a citizen." It gives us the English word *politics*. Paul affirmed that he was a loyal Jew who had lived as a good Jewish citizen and had not broken the Law. His conscience did not condemn him even though the Jews had condemned him.

"Conscience" is one of Paul's favorite words; he used it twice in Acts (23:1; 24:16) and twenty-one times in his letters. The word means "to know with, to know together." Conscience is the inner "judge" or "witness" that approves when we do right and disapproves when we do wrong (Rom. 2:15). Conscience does not *set* the standard; it only *applies* it. The conscience of a thief would bother him if he told the truth about his fellow crooks just as much as a Christian's conscience would convict him if he told a lie about his friends. Conscience does not make the standards; it only applies the standards of the person, whether they are good or bad, right or wrong.

Conscience may be compared to a window that lets in the light. God's Law is the light; and the cleaner the window is, the more the light shines in. As the window gets dirty, the light gets dimmer; and finally the light becomes darkness. A good conscience, or pure conscience (1 Tim. 3:9), is one that lets in God's light so that we are properly convicted if we do wrong and encouraged if we do right. A defiled conscience (1 Cor. 8:7) is one that has been sinned against so much that it is no longer dependable. If a person continues to sin against his conscience, he may end up with an evil conscience (Heb. 10:22) or a seared conscience (1 Tim. 4:2). Then he would feel convicted if he did what was *right* rather than what was wrong!

Paul had persecuted the church and had even caused innocent people to die, so how could he claim to have a good
conscience? *He had lived up to the light that he had*, and that
is all that a good conscience requires. After he became a
Christian and the bright light of God's glory shone into his
heart (2 Cor. 4:6), Paul then saw things differently and realized that he was "the chief of sinners" (1 Tim. 1:15).

Ananias the high priest (not to be confused with Annas in
4:6) was so incensed at Paul's saying that he had "lived in all
good conscience" that he ordered the nearest Jewish council
members to slap Paul across the mouth. (Jesus had been
treated in a similar way—John 18:22.) This was, of course,
illegal and inhumane; for, after all, Paul had not even been
proven guilty of anything. Certainly the high priest would be
expected to show honesty and fairness, if not compassion and
concern (Lev. 19:15; Heb. 5:2).

Paul responded with what appears to me to be justified
anger, although many disagree about this. When called to
account for what he had said, Paul did not apologize. Rather,
he showed respect for the *office* but not for the *man*. Ananias
was indeed one of the most corrupt men ever to be named
high priest. He stole tithes from the other priests and did all
he could to increase his authority. He was known as a brutal
man who cared more for Rome's favor than for Israel's wel-
fare.

In calling the high priest a "whited wall," Paul was simply
saying that the man was a hypocrite (Matt. 23:27; see Ezek.
13:10-12). Paul spoke prophetically, because God did indeed
smite this wicked man. When the Jews revolted against Rome
in the year 66, Ananias had to flee for his life because of his
known sympathies with Rome. The Jewish guerrillas found
him hiding in an aqueduct at Herod's palace, and they killed
him. It was an ignominious death for a despicable man.

Paul's reply in verse 5 has been variously interpreted. Some say that Paul did not know who the high priest was. Or perhaps Paul was speaking in holy sarcasm: "Could such a man actually be the high priest?" Since this was an informal meeting of the council, perhaps the high priest was not wearing his traditional garments and sitting in his usual place. For that matter, Paul had been away from the Jewish religious scene for many years and probably did not know many people in the council.

The quoting of Exodus 22:28 would indicate that Paul may not have known that it was the high priest who ordered him to be smitten. Again, note that Paul showed respect for the office, but not for the man who held the office. There is a difference.

Having failed in his personal approach, Paul then used a doctrinal approach. He declared that the real issue was his faith in the doctrine of the Resurrection, a doctrine over which the Pharisees and Sadducees violently disagreed. Paul knew that by defending this important doctrine, he would divide the council and soon have the members disputing among themselves, which is exactly what happened. So violent was the response that Claudius and his men had to rush down to the floor of the council chamber and rescue their prisoner for the second time!

Was Paul "playing politics" when he took this approach? I don't think so. After his unfortunate clash with the high priest, Paul realized that he could never get a fair trial before the Sanhedrin. If the trial had continued, he might well have been condemned and taken out and stoned as a blasphemer. The Asian Jews, if given opportunity to testify, could well have added fuel to the fire with their false witness. No, the wisest thing to do was to end the hearing as soon as possible and trust God to use the Roman legions to protect him from the Jews.

There is a second consideration: Paul was absolutely right

when he said that the real issue was the doctrine of the resurrection, not "the resurrection" in general, but the resurrection of Jesus Christ (see 24:21; 26:6-8; 28:20). Had he been given the opportunity, Paul would have declared the Gospel of "Jesus Christ and the Resurrection" just as he had declared it before Jewish congregations in many parts of the Empire. The witness in Acts centers on the Resurrection (see 1:22; 2:32; 3:15).

Jesus had stood trial before the Sanhedrin, and so had His apostles; and now Paul had witnessed to them. What great opportunities the council had and yet they would not believe!

2. Paul and the Lord Jesus (23:11)

A few years after Paul's conversion, when Paul's life was in danger in Jerusalem, Jesus appeared to him in the temple and told him what to do (22:17-21). When Paul was discouraged in Corinth and contemplated going elsewhere, Jesus appeared to him and encouraged him to stay (18:9-10). Now, when Paul was certainly at "low ebb" in his ministry, Jesus appeared once again to encourage and instruct him. Paul would later receive encouragement during the storm (27:22-25) and during his trial in Rome (2 Tim. 4:16-17). "Lo, I am with you always" is a great assurance for every situation (Matt. 28:20).

The Lord's message to Paul was one of *courage.* "Be of good cheer!" simply means "Take courage!" Jesus often spoke these words during His earthly ministry. He spoke them to the palsied man (Matt. 9:2) and to the woman who suffered with the hemorrhage (Matt. 9:22). He shouted them to the disciples in the storm (Matt. 14:27), and repeated them in the Upper Room (John 16:33). As God's people, we can always take courage in times of difficulty because the Lord is with us and will see us through.

It was also a message of *commendation.* The Lord did not rebuke Paul for going to Jerusalem. Rather, He commended him for the witness he had given, even though that witness had not been received. When you read the account of Paul's days in Jerusalem, you get the impression that everything Paul did failed miserably. His attempt to win over the legalistic Jews only helped cause a riot in the temple, and his witness before the Sanhedrin left the council in confusion. But the Lord was pleased with Paul's testimony, and that's what really counts.

Finally, it was a message of *confidence*: Paul would go to Rome! This had been Paul's desire for months (19:21; Rom. 15:22-29), but events in Jerusalem had made it look as though that desire would not be fulfilled. What encouragement this promise gave to Paul in the weeks that followed, difficult weeks when leaders lied about him, when fanatics tried to kill him, and when government officials ignored him. In all of this, the Lord was with him and fulfilling His perfect plan to get His faithful servant to Rome.

3. Paul and the Jewish Conspirators (23:12-35)

Paul's life had been in danger from the very beginning of his ministry, when he witnessed for Christ in Damascus (9:22-25). During his first visit to Jerusalem after his conversion, the Hellenistic Jews tried to kill him (9:29). The Jews drove him out of Antioch in Pisidia (13:50-51) and threatened to stone him in Iconium (14:5). Paul was stoned in Lystra (14:19-20); and in Corinth, the Jews tried to get him arrested (18:12-17). In Ephesus, the Jews had a plot to kill him (20:19), and they even planned to kill him at sea (20:3). Paul's words in 1 Thessalonians 2:14-16 take on special meaning when you consider all that Paul suffered at the hands of his own countrymen.

Perhaps it was the Asian Jews who conspired to kill Paul (21:27-29). Certain of the chief priests and elders agreed to cooperate with them and try to influence Claudius. It was a natural thing for the council to want further information from Paul, and it would have been an easy thing to ambush Paul's party and kill the apostle. If this got the captain in trouble with his superiors, the high priest could protect him. The Romans and the Jews had cooperated this way before (Matt. 28:11-15).

But the forty fasting men and the scheming religious leaders had forgotten that Paul was an apostle of Jesus Christ, and that the exalted Lord was watching from heaven. At Paul's conversion, the Lord had told him that he would suffer, but He had also promised that He would deliver him from his enemies (9:15-16; 26:16-17). Paul held on to that promise all of his life, and God was faithful.

We know nothing about Paul's sister and nephew except what is recorded here. Philippians 3:8 suggests that Paul lost his family when he became a Christian, but we do not know if any of his relatives were converted later. (The word "kinsman" in Rom. 16:7 and 11 means "fellow Jew," as in Rom. 9:3.) Since Paul's family had long been connected with the Pharisees (23:6), his sister was no doubt in touch with the "powers that be" and able to pick up the news that was passed along. Wives do chat with each other, and a secret is something you tell one person at a time!

It is not likely that either the sister or the nephew were believers, for that certainly would have shut them out of the official religious circle in Jerusalem. But they were devout Jews and knew that the plot was evil (Ex. 23:2). It was in the providence of God that they were able to hear the news and convey it privately to Claudius. St. Augustine said, "Trust the past to the mercy of God, the present to His love, and the future to His providence."

We certainly must admire the integrity and courage of Claudius Lysias, the captain. How did he know the boy was even telling the truth? Paul had already caused Claudius so much trouble that it might be a relief to get rid of him! The Jews did not know that Claudius was aware of their plot, so he could have used his "inside knowledge" for his own profit. No Roman soldier could afford to lose a prisoner, but there were always ways to work things out.

Throughout the Book of Acts, Dr. Luke speaks favorably of the Roman military officers, beginning with Cornelius in chapter 10 and ending with Julius (27:1, 3, 43). There is no record in Acts of *official* Roman persecution against the church; the opposition was instigated by the unbelieving Jews. While the Empire had its share of corrupt political opportunists, for the most part, the military leaders were men of quality who respected the Roman law.

Claudius' plan was simple and wise. He knew that he had to get Paul out of Jerusalem or there would be one murderous plot after another, and one of them just might succeed. He also knew that he had better determine the charges against Paul or he might be accused of illegally holding a Roman citizen. He could solve both problems by sending Paul to Caesarea and putting him under the authority of Felix, the Roman governor.

If Paul had been a private citizen, attempting to travel from Jerusalem to Caesarea (about sixty-five miles), he would have been an easy target for the conspirators. But God arranged for 470 Roman soldiers to protect him, almost half of the men in the temple garrison! Once again in his career, Paul was smuggled out of a city under cover of night (9:25; 17:10).

The captain's official letter is most interesting. Of course, Claudius put himself and his men in the best light, which is to be expected. While it is true they prevented Paul from being killed, it was not because they knew he was a Roman. Claudius thought Paul was an Egyptian and almost had him scourged!

Verse 29 is another of Luke's "official statements" from

Roman officials, proving that Christians were not considered criminals. The officials in Philippi had almost apologized to Paul (16:35-40), and Gallio in Corinth had refused to try him (18:14-15). In Ephesus, the town clerk told 25,000 people that the Christians were innocent of any crime (19:40), and now the Roman captain from the temple fortress was writing the same thing. Later, Festus (25:24-25) and Herod Agrippa (26:31-32) would also affirm that Paul should have been set free. Even the Jewish leaders in Rome had to confess that they had had no official news against Paul (28:21).

Leaving at 9 o'clock that night, Paul and his escort went from Jerusalem to Antiparis, about thirty-seven miles away. This must have been an all-night forced march for that many people to cover that much ground in that short a time. The cavalry then continued with Paul while the 200 soldiers returned to the barracks, since the dangerous part of the trip was now over. They traveled another twenty-seven miles to Caesarea where Paul was officially turned over to Felix. Paul was safe from the Jewish plotters, but was he safe from Felix?

Antonius Felix was governor (procurator) of Judea. He was married to Drusilla, a Jewess who was daughter of Herod Agrippa I (12:1) and who left her husband to become Felix's third wife. She was sister of Herod Agrippa II (25:13ff). The Roman historian Tacitus said that Felix "exercised the power of a king in the spirit of a slave." Felix was called "a vulgar ruffian" and lived up to the name.

Not only was Paul protected by an escort fit for a king, but he was put, not in the common prison, but in the palace built by Herod the Great, where the governor had his official headquarters. We wonder if any of the believers in Caesarea knew about Paul's presence and sought to bring him personal aid and encouragement. They would certainly remember the visit of Agabus and realize that his dire prophecy had been fulfilled (21:10-14).

As you review the events recorded in this chapter, you cannot help but be impressed with the commitment of the Apostle Paul to his calling. "None of these things move me!" (20:24) If ever a man dared to follow Christ, come what may, he was that man. Paul did not look for the easy way but for the way that would most honor the Lord and win the lost. He was even willing to become a prisoner if that would further the work of the Gospel.

You are also impressed with the amazing providence of God in caring for His servant. "The angel of the Lord encamps all around those who fear Him, and delivers them" (Ps. 34:7, NKJV). "Let us trust in God, and be very courageous for the Gospel," wrote Charles Spurgeon, "and the Lord Himself will screen us from all harm."

God's people can afford to be daring, in the will of God, because they know their Saviour will be dependable and work out His perfect will. Paul was alone—but not alone! His Lord was with him and he had nothing to fear. Like Paul, let us be daring!

10
Paul the Witness

Acts 24

"Law was the most characteristic and lasting expression of the Roman spirit," wrote historian Will Durant in *Caesar and Christ*. "The first person in Roman law was the citizen." In other words, it was the responsibility of the court to protect the citizen from the State; but too often various kinds of corruption infected the system and made justice difficult for the common man. Paul would soon discover how corrupt a Roman governor could be.

"The secret of Roman government was the principle of indirect rule," wrote Arnold Toynbee. This meant that the real burden of administration was left pretty much on the shoulders of the local authorities. Imperial Rome got involved only if there was danger from without or if the local governing units were at odds with one another.

In this chapter we see the Roman legal system at work and three men each making his contribution.

1. Tertullus: False Accusations (24:1-9)
In the Bible record, when people go *to* Jerusalem, they always

go up; but when they go *from* Jerusalem, they always go down. This explains why the official Jewish party "descended" when they came to Caesarea. With Ananias the high priest were some of the Jewish elders as well as a lawyer to present the case and defend their charges. Roman law was as complex as our modern law, and it took an expert to understand it and know how to apply it successfully to his client's case.

Tertullus began with the customary *flattery*, a normal part of the judicial routine. After all, before you can win your case, you must win over your judge. Tacitus, the Roman orator and politician, called flatterers "those worst of enemies"; and Solomon wrote that "a flattering mouth works ruin" (Prov. 26:28, NKJV).

The lawyer complimented Felix because the governor's many reforms had brought quietness to the land. (Question: Why did it require nearly 500 soldiers to protect one man in transit from Jerusalem to Caesarea?) It was true that Felix had put down some revolts, but he had certainly not brought peace to the land. In fact, during the time Felix was suppressing robbers in his realm, he was also hiring robbers to murder the high priest Jonathan! So much for his reforms.

But the prosecutor's accusations against Paul were no more truthful than his flattery. He brought three charges: a personal charge ("he is a pestilent fellow"), a political charge (sedition and leading an illegal religion), and a doctrinal charge (profaning the temple).

As for Paul being "a pest," it all depends on one's point of view. The Jews wanted to maintain their ancient traditions, and Paul was advocating something new. The Romans were afraid of anything that upset their delicate "peace" in the Empire, and Paul's record of causing trouble was long and consistent. As Vance Havner used to say, "Wherever Paul went, there was either a riot or a revival!"

This personal charge was based on the Jews' conflicts with Paul in different parts of the Roman world. I have already pointed out that it was his own countrymen, not the Roman authorities, who caused Paul trouble from city to city. The Jews from Asia (21:27) would certainly have stories to tell about Lystra, Corinth, and Ephesus! This first accusation reminds us of the charges brought against the Lord Jesus at His trial (Luke 23:1-2, 5).

The political charge was much more serious, because no Roman official wanted to be guilty of permitting illegal activities that would upset the "Pax Romana" (Roman Peace). Rome had given the Jews freedom to practice their religion, but the Roman officials kept their eyes on them lest they use their privileges to weaken the Empire. When Tertullus called Paul "an instigator of insurrections among all the Jews throughout the Roman Empire" (WUEST), he immediately got the attention of the governor. Of course, his statement was an exaggeration, but how many court cases have been won by somebody stretching the truth?

Tertullus knew that there was some basis for this charge because Paul had preached to the Jews that Jesus Christ was their King and Lord. To the Romans and the unbelieving Jews, this message sounded like treason against Caesar (Acts 16:20-21; 17:5-9). Furthermore, it was illegal to establish a new religion in Rome without the approval of the authorities. If Paul indeed was a "ringleader of the sect of the Nazarenes," then his enemies could easily build a case against him.

At that time, the Christian faith was still identified with the Jews, and they were permitted by the Romans to practice their religion. There had been Gentile seekers and God-fearers in the synagogues, so the presence of Gentiles in the churches did not create legal problems. Later, when the number of Gentile believers increased and more of the congregations separated from the Jewish synagogues, then Rome saw the difference between Jews and Christians and trouble began. Rome did not want a rival religion thriving in the Empire and creating problems.

Tertullus' third accusation had to be handled with care because it implicated a Roman officer who had saved a man's life. For the most part, Roman officials like Felix did not want anything to do with cases involving Jewish law (John 18:28-31; Acts 16:35-40; 18:12-17). The fewer Jews who ended up in Roman courts, the better it would be for the Empire. Tertullus had to present this third charge in a way that made the Jews look good without making the Romans look too bad, and he did a good job.

To begin with, he softened the charge. The accusation given by the Asian Jews was that Paul had polluted the temple (21:28), but Tertullus said, "He even tried to profane the temple" (v. 6, NKJV). Why the change? For at least two good reasons. To begin with, Paul's accusers realized that the original charge could never be substantiated if the facts were investigated. But even more, the Asian Jews who started the story seemed to have vanished from the scene! If there were no witnesses, there could be no evidence or conviction.

When you compare Luke's account of Paul's arrest (21:27-40) with the captain's account (23:25-30) and the lawyer's account (24:6-8), you can well understand why judges and juries can get confused. Tertullus gave the impression that Paul had actually been guilty of profaning the temple, that the Jews had been within their rights in seizing him, and that the captain had stepped out of line by interfering. It was Claudius, not the Jews, who was guilty of treating a Roman citizen with violence! But Felix had the official letter before him and was more likely to believe his captain than a paid Hellenistic Jewish lawyer.

Tertullus knew that the Jews had authority from Rome to arrest and prosecute those who violated Jewish law. True, the

Romans thought that the Jews' devotion to their traditions was excessive and superstitious; yet Rome wisely let them have their way. The Jews were even permitted to execute guilty offenders in capital cases, such as Paul's "offense" of permitting Gentiles to cross the protective barricade in the temple (21:28-29). Tertullus argued that if Claudius had not interfered, the Jews would have tried Paul themselves, and this would have saved Felix and Rome a great deal of trouble and expense.

In closing his argument, Tertullus hinted that Claudius Lysias should have been there personally and had not just sent the Jewish leaders to present the case. Why was he absent? Could he not defend his case? Was he trying to "pass the buck" to others? As far as we know, during the two years Paul was detained in Caesarea, Claudius never did show up to tell his side of the story. We wonder why.

But Paul was there and Felix could get the truth out of him! "If you examine Paul," the clever lawyer said, "you will find that what I am saying is true." The other members of the Jewish delegation united in agreeing with their lawyer, which was no surprise to anybody.

2. Paul: Faithful Answers (24:10-21)

But the governor did not examine Paul. He merely nodded his head as a signal that it was now Paul's turn to speak. Paul did not flatter Felix (see 1 Thes. 2:1-6); he merely acknowledged that the governor was a man of experience and therefore a man of knowledge. Felix knew about the "sect of the Nazarenes" (v. 22) and what the Jews were doing to it. After this brief but honest introduction, Paul then proceeded to answer the charges of Tertullus (vv. 10-16), the Asian Jews (vv. 17-19) and the Jewish council (vv. 20-21).

As far as the temple charge was concerned, Paul was in the temple to worship and not to lead a disturbance. In fact, the temple records would show that Paul was registered to pay the costs for four Jews who had taken a Nazirite vow. Paul had not preached in the temple or the synagogues, nor had he preached anywhere in the city. (Years before, Paul had made an agreement with Peter and the Jerusalem elders that he would not evangelize the Jews in Jerusalem. See Gal. 2:7-10.) Nobody could prove that he was guilty of leading any kind of rebellion against the Jews or the Romans.

Furthermore, since he had been in Jerusalem only a week (the twelve days of v. 11, minus the five days of v. 1), there had hardly been time to organize and lead an assault on the temple! While students of Paul's life do not agree on every detail, the order of events was probably something like this:

Day 1 —Paul arrived in Jerusalem (21:17)
Day 2 —Met with James and the elders (21:18)
Day 3 —In the temple with the Nazirites (21:26)
Day 4 —In the temple
Day 5 —In the temple
Day 6 —Arrested in the temple (21:27)
Day 7 —Met with the Jewish council (23:1-10)
Day 8 —Threatened; taken to Caesarea (23:12, 23)
Day 9 —Arrived in Caesarea (23:33)
Day 10—Waited (Felix sent for the Jewish leaders)
Day 11—Waited for the Jewish leaders to arrive
Day 12—Waited—they arrived—hearing scheduled
Day 13—The hearing conducted

The four men who had taken the Nazirite vow were evidently already involved in their temple duties when James suggested that Paul pay their costs (21:24). If they had started the day before Paul arrived in Jerusalem, then the day of Paul's arrest would have been the seventh day of their obligations (21:27). The *New American Standard Bible* translates

21:27, "And when the seven days were almost over." This implies that the events occurred on the seventh day of their schedule, Paul's sixth day in the city.

It would probably take two days for the official Roman messenger to get from Caesarea to Jerusalem, and another two days for Ananias and his associates to make it to Caesarea. They were not likely to linger; the case was too important.

Having disposed of the temple charges, Paul then dealt with the charges of sedition and heresy. Even though the high priest was a Sadducee, there were certainly Pharisees in the official Jewish delegation, so Paul appealed once again to their religious roots in the Scriptures. The fact that Paul was a Christian did not mean that he worshiped a different God from the God of his fathers. It only meant he worshiped the God of his fathers in a new and living way, for the only acceptable way to worship the Father is through Jesus Christ (John 5:23). His faith was still founded on the Old Testament Scriptures, and they bore witness to Jesus Christ.

The Sadducees accepted the five Books of Moses (the Law), but not the rest of the Old Testament. They rejected the doctrine of the Resurrection because they said it could not be found anywhere in what Moses wrote. (Jesus had refuted that argument, but they chose to ignore it. See Matthew 22:23-33.) By declaring his personal faith in the Resurrection, Paul affirmed his orthodox convictions and identified himself with the Pharisees. Once again, the Pharisees were caught on the horns of a dilemma, for if Paul's faith was that of a heretic, then they were heretics too!

Paul and the early Christians did not see themselves as "former Jews" but as "fulfilled Jews." The Old Testament was a new book to them because they had found their Messiah. They knew that they no longer needed the rituals of the Jewish Law in order to please God, but they saw in these ceremonies and ordinances a revelation of the Saviour. Both as a Pharisee and a Christian, Paul had "taken pains" always to have a good conscience and to seek to please the Lord.

Having replied to the false charges of Tertullus, Paul then proceeded to answer the false accusation of the Asian Jews that he had profaned the temple (vv. 17-19). He had not come to Jerusalem to defile the temple but to bring needed help to the Jewish people and to present his own offerings to the Lord. (This is the only mention in Acts of the special offering.) When the Asians saw him in the temple, he was with four men who were fulfilling their Nazirite vows. How could Paul possibly be *worshiping* God and *profaning* God's house at the same time? A Jewish priest was in charge of Paul's temple activities; so, if the holy temple was defiled, the priest was responsible. Paul was only obeying the Law.

Now Paul reached the heart of his defense, for it was required by Roman law that the accusers face the accused at the trial, or else the charges would be dropped. Ananias had wisely not brought any of the Hellenistic Jews with him, for he was sure that their witness would fall down under official examination. These men were good at inciting riots; they were not good at producing facts.

Paul closed his defense by replying to the members of the Jewish council (vv. 20-21). Instead of giving him a fair hearing, the high priest and the Sanhedrin had abused him and refused to hear him out. Ananias was no doubt grateful that Paul said nothing about his slap in the face, for it was not legal for a Roman citizen to be treated that way.

Do we detect a bit of holy sarcasm in Paul's closing statement? We might paraphrase it, "If I have done anything evil, it is probably this: I reminded the Jewish council of our great Jewish doctrine of the Resurrection." Remember, the Book of Acts is a record of the early church's witness to the resurrection of Jesus Christ (1:22). The Sadducees had long abandoned the doctrine, and the Pharisees did not give it the practical importance it deserved. Of course, Paul would have related this doctrine to the resurrection of Jesus Christ, and the Sanhedrin did not want that.

They had accused Paul of being anti-Jewish and anti-Roman, but they could not prove their charges. If the Jewish leaders had further pursued any of these charges, their case would have collapsed. But there was enough circumstantial evidence to plant doubts in the minds of the Roman officials, and perhaps there was enough race prejudice in them to water that seed and encourage it to grow. After all, had not the Emperor Claudius expelled the Jews from Rome? (18:2) Perhaps Paul would bear watching.

3. Felix: Foolish Attitudes (24:22-27)

If ever a man failed both personally and officially, that man was Felix, procurator of Judea. He certainly could not plead ignorance of the facts, because he was "well acquainted with the Way" (v. 22, NIV). His wife, Drusilla, was a Jewess and perhaps kept him informed of the activities among her people, and as a Roman official, he would carefully (if privately) investigate these things. He saw the light, but he preferred to live in the darkness.

Felix saw to it that Paul was comfortably cared for while at the same time safely guarded. "Liberty" in verse 23 means that he was not put in the common jail or kept in close confinement. He had limited freedom in the palace, chained to a soldier. (The guards were changed every six hours, a perfect captive congregation!) Paul's friends were permitted to minister to him (Greek: "wait on him as personal servants"), so people could come and go to meet his needs. What Paul's ministry was during those two years in Caesarea, we do not know, but we can be sure he gave a faithful witness for the Lord.

The record of one such witness is given by Luke, and it makes Felix's guilt even greater. Not only was Felix's mind informed, but his heart was moved by fear, and yet he would not obey the truth. It is not enough for a person to know the facts about Christ, or to have an emotional response to a message. He or she must willingly repent of sin and trust the Saviour. "But you are not willing to come to Me that you may have life" (John 5:40, NKJV).

It must have been the curiosity of his wife, Drusilla, that prompted Felix to give Paul another hearing. She wanted to hear Paul; for, after all, her family had been involved with "the Way" on several occasions. Her great-grandfather tried to kill Jesus in Bethlehem (Matt. 2); her great-uncle killed John the Baptist and mocked Jesus (Luke 23:6-12); and Acts 12:1-2 tells of her father killing the Apostle James.

Dr. Luke has given us only the three points of Paul's sermon to this infamous couple: righteousness, self-control, and the judgment to come. But what an outline! Paul gave them three compelling reasons why they should repent and believe on Jesus Christ.

First, they had to do something about *yesterday's sin* ("righteousness"). In 1973, Dr. Karl Menninger, one of the world's leading psychiatrists, published a startling book, *Whatever Became of Sin?* He pointed out that the very word *sin* has gradually dropped out of our vocabulary, "the word, along with the notion." We talk about mistakes, weaknesses, inherited tendencies, faults, and even errors; but we do not face up to the fact of sin.

"People are no longer sinful," said Phyllis McGinley, noted American writer and poet. "They are only immature or underprivileged or frightened or, more particularly, sick." But a holy God demands righteousness; that's the bad news. Yet the good news is that this same holy God *provides* His own righteousness to those who trust Jesus Christ (Rom. 3:21-26). We can never be saved by our own righteousness of good works. We can be saved only through Christ's righteousness made available by His finished work of salvation on the cross.

The second point in Paul's sermon dealt with self-control: we must do something about *today's temptations*. Man can control almost everything but himself. Here were Felix and Drusilla, prime illustrations of lack of self-control. She divorced her husband to become Felix's third wife, and though a Jewess, she lived as though God had never given the Ten Commandments at Sinai. Felix was an unscrupulous official who did not hesitate to lie, or even to murder, in order to get rid of his enemies and promote himself. Self-control was something neither of them knew much about.

Paul's third point was the clincher: "judgment to come." *We must do something about tomorrow's judgment.* Perhaps Paul told Felix and Drusilla what he told the Greek philosophers: God has "appointed a day, in which He will judge the world in righteousness" by the Lord Jesus Christ (17:31). Jesus Christ is either your Saviour or your Judge. How do we know that Jesus Christ is the Judge? "He has given assurance of this to all by raising Him from the dead" (17:31, NKJV). Once again, the resurrection!

"Felix trembled" (v. 25), which literally means, "Felix became terrified." Roman leaders prided themselves in their ability to be stoical and restrain their emotions under all circumstances, but a conviction from God gripped Felix's heart, and he could not hide it. Paul had diagnosed the case and offered the remedy. It was up to Felix to receive it.

What did Felix do? *He procrastinated!* "When I have a convenient time, I will call for you," he told the apostle. "Procrastination is the thief of time," wrote Edward Young. Perhaps he was thinking about the English proverb, "One of these days is none of these days." Procrastination is also the thief of souls. The most "convenient season" for a lost sinner to be saved is *right now*. "Behold, now is the accepted time; behold, now is the day of salvation" (2 Cor. 6:2).

"I think there's a special time for each person to be saved," a man argued to whom I was witnessing. "I can't get saved until that time comes."

"What are the signals that your special time has come?" I asked.

"Well," he drawled, "I don't rightly know."

"Then how will you know when you are supposed to be saved?" I asked. But the stupidity of his position never bothered him. I do hope he was saved before he died.

Consider Felix's foolish attitudes. He had a foolish attitude toward God's Word, thinking that he could "take it or leave it." But God "now *commands* all men everywhere to repent" (17:30, NKJV, italics mine). When God speaks, men and women had better listen and obey.

Felix had a foolish attitude toward his sins. He knew he was a sinner, yet he refused to break with his sins and obey the Lord. He had a foolish attitude toward God's grace. The Lord had been long-suffering toward Felix, yet the governor would not surrender. Felix was not sure of another day's life, yet he foolishly procrastinated. "Do not boast about tomorrow, for you do not know what a day may bring forth" (Prov. 27:1, NIV).

Instead of listening to Paul, Felix tried to "use" Paul as a political pawn, either to get money from the church or to gain favor with the Jews. The fact that Felix had further discussions with Paul is no indication that his heart was interested in spiritual things. Paul's friends were coming and going, and perhaps some of them had access to the large offering sent by the Gentile churches. Certainly Paul gave further witness to the governor, but to no avail. When Felix was replaced, he left Paul a prisoner, but it was Felix who was really the prisoner.

The governor's mind was enlightened (v. 22), his emotions were stirred (v. 25), but his will would not yield. He tried to gain the world, but, as far as we know, he lost his soul. He procrastinated himself into hell.

Dr. Clarence Macartney told a story about a meeting in hell. Satan called his four leading demons together and commanded them to think up a new lie that would trap more souls.

"I have it!" one demon said. "I'll go to earth and tell people there is no God."

"It will never work," said Satan. "People can look around them and see that there is a God."

"I'll go and tell them there is no heaven!" suggested a second demon, but Satan rejected that idea. "Everybody knows there is life after death and they want to go to heaven."

"Let's tell them there is no hell!" said a third demon.

"No, conscience tells them their sins will be judged," said the devil. "We need a better lie than that."

Quietly, the fourth demon spoke. "I think I've solved your problem," he said. "I'll go to earth and tell everybody *there is no hurry.*"

The best time to trust Jesus Christ is—*now!*

And the best time to tell others the good news of the Gospel is—*now!*

11

Paul the Defender

Acts 25–26

The new governor, Porcius Festus, was a better man than his predecessor and took up his duties with the intention of doing what was right. However, he soon discovered that Jewish politics was not easy to handle, especially the two-year-old case of the Apostle Paul, a prisoner with no official charges against him. Paul was a Jew whose countrymen wanted to kill him, and he was a Roman whose government did not know what to do with him.

What a dilemma! If Festus released Paul, the Jews would cause trouble, and that was something the new governor dared not risk. However, if he held Paul prisoner, Festus would have to explain why a Roman citizen was being held without definite official charges. Festus knew that it was smart for him to act quickly and take advantage of the fact that he was a newcomer on the scene. To delay would only make the problem worse, and it was bad enough already.

These two chapters present Festus in three different situations, each of which related to the Apostle Paul.

1. Conciliation: Festus and the Jewish Leaders (25:1-12)
Knowing how important it was for him to get along well with
the Jewish leaders, Festus lost no time in visiting the holy city
and paying his respects; and the leaders lost no time in bringing up Paul's case. The new high priest was Ishmael; he had
replaced Jonathan who had been killed by Felix. Ishmael
wanted to resurrect the plot of two years before and remove
Paul once and for all (23:12-15).

It is not likely that the new governor knew anything about
the original plot or even suspected that the Jewish religious
leaders were out for blood. Since a Roman court could meet
in Jerusalem as well as in Caesarea, transferring Paul would
be a normal procedure. Festus would probably not demand
that a large retinue go with him, so an ambush would be
easy. Finally, since it was a matter involving a Jewish prisoner
and the Jewish law, the logical place to meet would be
Jerusalem.

"Kill Paul!" had been the cry of the unbelieving Jews ever
since Paul had arrived in Jerusalem (21:27-31; 22:22; 23:10-
15; 25:3); however, Festus knew nothing of this. Paul had
been warned of this danger, but he had also been assured
that the Lord would protect him, use his witness and then
take him safely to Rome (23:11; 26:17). The situation was
growing more serious, for now it was the council itself, and
not a group of outsiders, that was plotting Paul's death. You
would think that their anger would have subsided after two
years, but it had not. Satan the murderer was hard at work
(John 8:44).

Festus was wise not to cooperate with their scheme, but he
did invite the leaders to accompany him to Caesarea and face
Paul once again. This would give Festus opportunity to review
the case and get more facts. The Jews agreed, but the hearing
brought out nothing new. The Jewish delegation (this time
without their lawyer) only repeated the same unfounded and

unproved accusations, hoping that the governor would agree with them and put Paul to death (25:15-16).

What did Paul do? He once again affirmed that he was innocent of any crime against the Jewish law, the temple, or the Roman government. Festus saw that no progress was being made, so he asked Paul if he would be willing to be tried in Jerusalem. He did this to please the Jews and probably did not realize that he was jeopardizing the life of his famous prisoner. But a Roman judge could not move a case to another court without the consent of the accused, *and Paul refused to go!* Instead, he claimed the right of every Roman citizen to appeal to Caesar.

What led Paul to make that wise decision? For one thing, he knew that his destination was Rome, not Jerusalem; and the fastest way to get there was to appeal to Caesar. Paul also knew that the Jews had not given up their hopes of killing him, so he was wise to stay under the protection of Rome. By appealing to Caesar, Paul forced the Romans to guard him and take him to Rome. Finally, Paul realized that he could never have a fair trial in Jerusalem anyway, so why go?

It must have infuriated the Jewish leaders when Paul, by one statement, took the case completely out of their hands. He made it clear that he was willing to die *if* he could be proved guilty of a capital crime, but first they had to find him guilty. Festus met with his official council, and they agreed to send Paul to Nero for trial. No doubt the new governor was somewhat embarrassed that he had handled one of his first cases so badly that the prisoner was forced to appeal to Caesar; and to Caesar he must go!

2. Consultation: Festus and Agrippa (25:13-22)

But the new governor's problems were not over. He had managed not to offend the Jews, but he had not determined the legal charges against his prisoner. How could he send such a notable prisoner to the emperor and not have the man's crimes listed against him?

About that time, Festus had a state visit from Herod Agrippa II and Herod's sister, Bernice. This youthful king, the last of the Herodians to rule, was the great-grandson of the Herod who killed the Bethlehem babes, and the son of the Herod who killed the Apostle James (Acts 12). The fact that his sister lived with him created a great deal of suspicion on the part of the Jewish people, for their Law clearly condemned incest (Lev. 18:1-18; 20:11-21). Rome had given Herod Agrippa II legal jurisdiction over the temple in Jerusalem, so it was logical that Festus share Paul's case with him.

Festus was smart enough to understand that the Jewish case against Paul had nothing to do with civil law. It was purely a matter of "religious questions" (18:14-15; 23:29) which the Romans were unprepared to handle, especially the doctrine of the Resurrection. Verse 19 proves that Paul was defending much more than the resurrection in general. He was declaring and defending the resurrection of Jesus Christ. As we have noted in our studies, this is the key emphasis of the witness of the church in the Book of Acts.

Festus gave the impression that he wanted to move the trial to Jerusalem because the "Jewish questions" could be settled only by Jewish people in Jewish territory (v. 20). It was a pure fabrication, of course, because his real reason was to please the Jewish leaders, most of whom King Herod knew. Festus needed something definite to send to the emperor Nero, and perhaps Agrippa could supply it. ("Augustus" in vv. 21 and 25 is a title, "the august one," and not a proper name.)

The king was an expert in Jewish matters (26:2-3) and certainly would be keenly interested in knowing more about this man who caused a riot in the temple. Perhaps Herod could assist Festus in finding out the real charges against Paul, and perhaps Festus could assist Herod in learning more about Jewish affairs in the holy city.

3. Confrontation: Festus, Agrippa, and Paul (25:23–26:32)

It seems incredible that all of this pomp and ceremony was because of one little Jewish man who preached the Gospel of Jesus Christ! But the Lord had promised Paul he would bear witness before "Gentiles and kings" (9:15), and that promise was being fulfilled again. Once Paul was finished with his witness, all his hearers would know how to be saved and would be without excuse.

They met in an "audience room" in the palace, and the key military men and officers of the Roman government were there. Paul's case had probably been discussed by various official people many times over the past two years, so very few of those present were ignorant of the affair.

Festus was certainly exaggerating when he said that "all the multitude of the Jews" had pressed charges against Paul, but that kind of statement would make the Jews present feel much better. Verse 25 gives us the second of Luke's "official statements" declaring Paul's innocence (see 23:29); and there will be others before his book is completed.

In his flowery speech before Agrippa, Festus indicated that he wanted the king to examine Paul (v. 26), but there is no record that he did. In fact, before the session ended, Paul became the judge, and Festus, King Agrippa, and Bernice became the defendants! Paul was indeed defending himself (26:24, NKJV), but at the same time, he was presenting the truth of the Gospel and witnessing to the difference Jesus Christ can make in a person's life. This is the longest of Paul's speeches found in Acts.

King Agrippa was in charge and told Paul that he was free to speak. In his brief introduction, Paul sincerely gave thanks that Agrippa was hearing his case, because he knew the king was an expert in Jewish religious matters. Paul did not mention it then, but he also knew that the king believed the Old Testament prophets (v. 27). Paul also hinted that his speech might be a long one and that he would appreciate the king's patience in hearing him out.

Five key statements summarize Paul's defense.

(1) *"I lived a Pharisee"* (vv. 4-11). Paul's early life in Jerusalem was known to the Jews, so there was no need to go into great detail. He was a devout Pharisee (Phil. 3:5) and the son of a Pharisee (Acts 23:6), and his peers had likely realized he would accomplish great things as a rabbi (Gal. 1:13-14, NIV). It was because of his convictions about the Resurrection and "the hope of Israel" that he was now a prisoner (see 23:6 and 24:15). Once again, Paul appealed to Jewish orthodoxy and loyalty to the Hebrew tradition.

It is worth noting that Paul mentioned "our twelve tribes" (v. 7). While it is true that the ten northern tribes (Israel) were conquered by Assyria in 722 B.C. and assimilated to some extent, it is not true that these ten tribes were "lost" or annihilated. Jesus spoke about all twelve tribes (Matt. 19:28), and so did James (James 1:1) and the Apostle John (Rev. 7:4-8 and 21:12). God knows where His chosen people are, and He will fulfill the promises He has made to them.

The pronoun *you* in verse 8 is plural, so Paul must have looked around at the entire audience as he spoke. The Greeks and Romans, of course, would not believe in the doctrine of the Resurrection (17:31-32), nor would the Sadducees who were present (23:8). To Paul, this was a crucial doctrine, for if there is no Resurrection, then Jesus Christ was not raised and Paul had no Gospel to preach. (For Paul's argument about the Resurrection and the Gospel, see 1 Cor. 15).

Paul was not only a Pharisee, but he had also been a zealous persecutor of the church. He had punished the believers and tried to force them to deny Jesus Christ, and some of them he had helped send to their death. The phrase "gave my voice" (v. 10) literally means "registered my vote." This suggests that Paul had been an official member of the Sanhedrin, but surely if that were true, seemingly he would have mentioned it in one of his speeches. The phrase probably means nothing more than he "voted against them" as a special representative of the high priest (9:2, 14).

In the early days of the church, the Jewish believers continued to meet in the synagogues, and that was where Paul found them and punished them (Matt. 10:17 and 23:34). What Paul in his early years looked upon as "religious zeal" (Gal. 1:13-14), in his later years he considered to be "madness" (v. 11). Like a wild animal, he had "made havoc of the church" (8:3), "breathing out threatenings and slaughter" (9:1).

(2) *"I saw a light"* (vv. 12-13). Not content to limit his work to Jerusalem, Paul had asked for authority to visit the synagogues in distant cities. His zeal had driven out many of the believers and they had taken their message to Jews in other communities (8:4).

Paul considered himself an enlightened man; for, after all, he was a Jew (Rom. 9:4-5), a scholar (22:3), and a Pharisee. In reality, Paul had lived in gross spiritual darkness. He knew the Law in his preconversion days, but he had not realized that the purpose of the Law was to bring him to Christ (Gal. 3:24). He had been a self-righteous Pharisee who needed to discover that his good works and respectable character could never save him and take him to heaven (Phil. 3:1-11).

The light that Paul saw was supernatural, for it was the glory of God revealed from heaven (compare 7:2 and 7:55-56). It actually had blinded Paul for three days (9:8-9), but his spiritual eyes had been opened to behold the living Christ (2 Cor. 4:3-6). But seeing a light was not enough; he also had to hear the Word of God.

(3) *"I heard a voice"* (vv. 14-18). Paul's companions had seen the light, but not the Lord; and they had heard a sound, but they could not understand the words. They all fell to the earth, but only Paul remained there (9:7). Jesus Christ spoke to Paul in the familiar Aramaic tongue of the Jews, called him by name, and told him it was futile for him to continue fighting the Lord. In that moment, Paul had made two surprising discoveries: Jesus of Nazareth was alive, and He was so united to His people that their suffering was His suffering! Paul was persecuting not only the church, but also his own Messiah!

How encouraging it is to know that God in His grace speaks to those who are His enemies. God had been dealing with Paul, but Paul had been resisting Him, kicking against the "goads." What were these "goads"? Certainly the testimony and death of Stephen (22:20), plus the faithful witness of the other saints who had suffered because of Paul. Perhaps Paul had also struggled with the emptiness and weakness of Judaism and his own inability to meet the demands of the Law. Even though he could now say he was "blameless" in conduct and conscience (Phil. 3:6; Acts 23:1), yet within his own heart, he certainly knew how far short he came of meeting God's holy standards (Rom. 7:7-16).

The word *minister* in verse 16 means "an under-rower" and refers to a lowly servant on a galley ship. Paul had been accustomed to being an honored leader, but after his conversion he became a subordinate worker; and Jesus Christ became his Master. The Lord had promised to be with Paul and protect him; and He also promised to reveal Himself to him. Paul saw the Lord on the Damascus Road, and again three years later while in the temple (22:17-21). Later, the Lord appeared to him in Corinth (18:9) and in Jerusalem (23:11), and He would appear to him again.

No doubt it was a surprise to Paul after his conversion to

hear that the Lord was sending him to the Gentiles. He had a great love for his own people and would gladly have lived and died to win them to Christ (Rom. 9:1-3), but that was not God's plan. He would always be "the apostle to the Gentiles."

Verse 18 describes both the spiritual condition of the lost and the gracious provision of Christ for those who will believe. You will find parallels in Isaiah 35:5, 42:6ff, and 61:1. The lost sinner is like a blind prisoner in a dark dungeon, and only Christ can open his eyes and give him light and freedom (2 Cor. 4:3-6). But even after he is set free, what about his court record and his guilt? The Lord forgives his sins and wipes the record clean! He then takes him into His own family as His own child and shares His inheritance with him!

What must the sinner do? He must trust Jesus Christ ("faith that is in Me"—v. 18). Paul had to lose his religion to gain salvation! He discovered in a moment of time that all of his righteousnesses were but filthy rags in God's sight, and that he needed the righteousness of Christ (Isa. 64:6).

(4) *"I was not disobedient"* (vv. 19-21). When Paul had asked, "Lord, what wilt Thou have me to do?" (9:6) he meant it sincerely; and when the Lord told him, he obeyed orders immediately. He began right at Damascus and it almost cost him his life (9:20-25). Likewise, when he had witnessed to the Jews in Jerusalem, they attempted to kill him (9:29-30). In spite of repeated discouragements and dangers, Paul had remained obedient to the call and the vision that Jesus Christ gave him. Nothing moved him! (20:24)

In verse 21, Paul clearly explained to Agrippa and Festus what had really happened in the temple and why it had happened. It was "on account of these things" that Paul had been attacked and almost killed: his declaration that Jesus of Nazareth was alive and was Israel's Messiah, his ministry to the Gentiles, and his offer of God's covenant blessings to both

Jews and Gentiles *on the same terms of repentance and faith* (see 20:21). The proud nationalistic Israelites would have nothing to do with a Jew who treated Gentiles like Jews!

(5) *"I continue unto this day"* (vv. 22-32). It is one thing to have a great beginning, with visions and voices, but quite another thing to keep on going, especially when the going is tough. The fact that Paul continued was proof of his conversion and evidence of the faithfulness of God. He was saved by God's grace and enabled to serve by God's grace (1 Cor. 15:10).

The one word that best summarizes Paul's life and ministry is "witnessing" (see v. 16). He simply shared with others what he had learned and experienced as a follower of Jesus Christ. His message was not something he manufactured, for it was based solidly on the Old Testament Scriptures. We must remind ourselves that Paul and the other apostles did not have the New Testament, but used the Old Testament to lead sinners to Christ and to nurture the new believers.

Verse 23 is a summary of the Gospel (1 Cor. 15:3-4), and each part can be backed up from the Old Testament. See, for example, Isaiah 52:13–53:12 and Psalm 16:8-11. Paul could even defend his call to the Gentiles from Isaiah 49:6 (see also Acts 13:47). Jesus was not the first person to be raised from the dead, but He was the first one to be raised and never die again. He is "the firstfruits of them that slept" (1 Cor. 15:20).

In his message in the temple, when Paul got to the word *Gentiles*, the crowd exploded (22:21-22). That is the word Paul spoke when Festus responded and loudly accused Paul of being mad. How strange that Festus did not think Paul was mad when he was persecuting the church! (v. 11) Nobody called D.L. Moody crazy when he was energetically selling shoes and making money, but when he started winning souls, people gave him the nickname "Crazy Moody." This was not the first time Paul had been called "crazy" (2 Cor. 5:13), and he was only following in the footsteps of his Master (Mark 3:20-21; John 10:20).

Paul had been addressing King Agrippa, but the emotional interruption of the governor forced him to reply. He reminded Festus that the facts about the ministry of Jesus Christ, including His death and resurrection, were public knowledge and "not done in a corner." The Jewish Sanhedrin was involved and so was the Roman governor, Pilate. Jesus of Nazareth had been a famous public figure for at least three years, and huge crowds had followed Him. How then could the governor plead ignorance?

Festus had not interrupted because he really thought Paul was mad. Had that been the case, he would have treated Paul gently and ordered some of his guards to escort him to a place of rest and safety. Furthermore, what official would send a raving madman to be tried before the emperor? No, the governor was only giving evidence of conviction in his heart. Paul's words had found their mark, and Festus was trying to escape.

But Paul did not forget King Agrippa, a Jew who was an expert in these matters. When Paul asked if Agrippa believed the prophets, he was forcing him to take a stand. Certainly the king would not repudiate what every Jew believed! But Agrippa knew that if he affirmed his faith in the prophets, he must then face the question, "Is Jesus of Nazareth the one about whom the prophets wrote?"

Festus avoided decision by accusing Paul of being mad. King Agrippa eluded Paul's question (and the dilemma it presented) by adopting a superior attitude and belittling Paul's witness. His reply in verse 28 can be stated, "Do you think that in such a short time, with such few words, you can persuade *me* to become a Christian?" Perhaps he spoke with a smirk on his face and a sneer in his voice. But he certainly spoke his own death warrant (John 3:18-21, 36).

Paul was polite in his reply. "I would to God, that whether in a short or long time, not only you, but also all who hear me this day, might become such as I am, except for these chains" (v. 29, NASB). Festus and Agrippa knew that their prisoner had a compassionate concern for them, and they could not easily escape his challenge. The best thing to do was to end the hearing, so the king stood up; and this told everybody that the audience was over.

Both Agrippa and Festus declared that Paul was innocent of any crime deserving of death. Luke continues to accumulate these official statements so that his readers will understand that Paul was an innocent man. (See 16:35-40; 18:12-17; 23:29; 25:25.) In fact, Paul might have been set free, had he not appealed to Caesar. Was he foolish in making his appeal? No, he was not, for it was the appeal to Caesar that finally ended the repeated accusations of the Jewish leaders. They knew they could not successfully fight against Rome.

What Agrippa and Festus did not understand was that *Paul* had been the judge and *they* had been the prisoners on trial. They had been shown the light and the way to freedom, but they had deliberately closed their eyes and returned to their sins. Perhaps they felt relieved that Paul would go to Rome and trouble them no more. The trial was over, but their sentence was still to come; and come it would.

What a wonderful thing is the opportunity to trust Jesus Christ and be saved! What a terrible thing is wasting that opportunity and perhaps never having another.

12

Paul Arrives in Rome

Acts 27–28

"I must also see Rome!" Those were Paul's words during his ministry in Ephesus (19:21), and little did he realize all that would happen to him before he would arrive in the Imperial city: illegal arrest, Roman and Jewish trials, confinement, and even shipwreck. He had long wanted to preach the Gospel in Rome (Rom. 1:14-16) and then go on into Spain (Rom. 15:28), but he had not planned to travel as a prisoner. Through it all, Paul trusted God's promise that he would witness in Rome (23:11); and the Lord saw him through.

Why would Luke devote such a long section of his book to a description of a voyage and shipwreck? Surely he could have summarized the account for us! But Luke was a skilled writer, inspired by the Spirit of God, and he knew what he was doing. For one thing, this exciting report balances the speeches that we have been reading and brings more drama into the account. Also, Luke was an accurate historian who presented the important facts about his hero and his voyage to Rome.

But perhaps the major purpose Luke had in mind was the presenting of Paul as the courageous leader who could take command of a difficult situation in a time of great crisis. Future generations would love and appreciate Paul all the more for what he did en route to Rome.

Since ancient times, writers have pictured life as a journey or a voyage. *Pilgrim's Progress* by John Bunyan is based on this theme, and so is Homer's *Odyssey*. We sometimes use the "voyage" metaphor in everyday conversation: "Smooth sailing!" or "Don't make shipwreck!" or "Sink or swim!" When a Christian dies, we might say, "She has reached the other shore." Dr. Luke was certainly not writing an allegory, but he did use this exciting event to show how one man's faith can make a big difference for him and others "in the storms of life." What an encouragement to our own faith!

In Paul's journey to Rome, we see the great apostle in four important roles.

1. Paul the Counselor (27:1-20)

Luke had not included himself since 21:18, but now he joined Paul and Aristarchus (19:29; 20:2, 4) for the voyage to Rome. It is possible that Luke was allowed to go as Paul's physician and Aristarchus as Paul's personal attendant. How Paul must have thanked God for his faithful friends who gave up their liberty, and even risked their lives, that he might have the help he needed. There is no evidence that either of these men had been arrested, yet Paul referred to Aristarchus as a "fellow prisoner" (Col. 4:10). This could refer to a voluntary imprisonment on his part in order to assist Paul.

Paul was not the only prisoner that Julius and his men were taking to Rome, for there were "certain other prisoners" with them. The Greek word means "others of a different kind" and may suggest that, unlike Paul, these men were going to Rome to die and not to stand trial. What mercy that they met Paul who could tell them how to go to heaven when they died!

The centurion found a coastal ship leaving Caesarea, so they embarked and covered the eighty miles from Caesarea to Sidon in one day. In Sidon, Paul was permitted to visit his friends and put together the things needed for the long trip. Luke records the kindness of a Roman officer to the Apostle Paul (24:23), as well as the encouragement of the anonymous believers in Sidon. Their names are in God's book and they shall be rewarded one day (Phil. 4:3).

From Sidon to Myra, the voyage became difficult because of the westerly winds. At Myra, Julius, a Roman officer, found a ship going to Italy; so he abandoned the slower coastal ship and put Paul and the others on board this large grain ship from Egypt that carried 276 passengers (vv. 37-38). Rome depended on Egypt for much of its grain supply, and the Roman government gave special consideration to those who ran these ships.

The strong winds again hindered their progress so that "many days" were required to cover the 130 miles from Myra to Cnidus. The pilot then steered south-southwest to Crete, passing Salmone and finally struggling into Fair Havens. It had been a most difficult voyage, a portent of things to come.

The centurion now had to decide whether to winter at Fair Havens or set sail and try to reach the port of Phoenix (Phoenicia, v. 12) on the southern coast of Crete, about forty miles away. His approach to making this decision is a classic illustration of how *not* to determine the will of God.

Paul admonished them to stay in Fair Havens. They had already encountered adverse winds, and it was now the start of the stormy season. "The fast" refers to the Day of Atonement, which fell in September/October; and every sailor knew that sailing was difficult from mid-September to mid-November, and impossible from mid-November to February.

Verse 10 sounds so much like a prophecy that we are prone to believe God gave Paul a premonition of danger. Paul had already experienced three shipwrecks (2 Cor. 11:25), so he was certainly speaking from experience. (The Greek word translated *perceive* in verse 10 means "to perceive from past experience.") However, the men in charge gave little value to Paul's warning, an attitude they lived to regret.

What were the factors that governed Julius' decision? To begin with, Fair Havens was not a comfortable place to settle down because it was too open to the winter storms. Phoenix had a more sheltered harbor. Julius also listened to the "expert advice" of the pilot and captain ("master and owner") of the ship. They advised that the ship head for Phoenix as fast as possible. Surely they could cover forty miles safely, and already they had lost too much time (v. 9). When Julius added up the votes, it was three to one that the ship set sail. After all, the majority cannot be wrong, especially when it includes the experts!

But the clinching argument came with an encouraging change in the weather, for the south wind began to blow gently, and that was just what they needed. As the ship left the harbor, perhaps Julius, the pilot, and the captain smiled tolerantly at Paul and his two friends as if to say, "See, you were wrong!"

However, it was not long before Paul was proved right, for the "soft wind" became a stormy wind. The word translated *tempestuous* gives us the English word *typhoon*. Sailors called this special wind "Euroclydon," a hybrid Greek and Latin word that means "a northeasterner." The crew had to let the ship drift because it was impossible to steer it, and the wind drove it twenty-three miles to the south, to the island of Cauda. Here the sailors pulled in the small boat that was towed behind larger ships, lest they lose it or it be driven against the ship and cause damage.

As the storm grew worse, the crew did all it could to keep the ship afloat. They wrapped ropes (or chains) around the hull so the boat would not come apart, and they took down some of the sails. The second day, they started throwing some of the wheat overboard, and the third day they jettisoned the furnishings. (Note Luke's use of "we" in v. 19.) Because of the storm, they could not see the sun or the stars, so it was impossible to determine their position. The situation seemed hopeless, and it all happened because one man would not listen to God's messenger.

Sometimes we get ourselves into storms for the same reasons: impatience (v. 9), accepting expert advice that is contrary to God's will, following the majority, and trusting "ideal" conditions (v. 13). "He that believeth shall not make haste" (Isa. 28:16). It pays to listen to God's Word.

2. Paul the Encourager (27:21-44)

"Paul began as a prisoner," said Joseph Parker; "he ended as the captain." Paul "took over" the situation when it was obvious that nobody else knew what to do. A crisis does not make a person; a crisis shows what a person is made of, and it tends to bring true leadership to the fore. Paul gently rebuked the centurion, pilot, and captain for ignoring his warning. Soon they would discover that God had spared all of them only because of Paul.

Consider Paul's four ministries of encouragement to the passengers and crew.

He shared God's Word with them (vv. 22-26). A messenger from the Lord had visited Paul and told him that the ship and cargo would be lost, but that all the passengers would be spared and cast upon an island. Once again, the Lord gave him a special word of encouragement at the right time (18:9-10; 23:11). Today, we are not likely to have visions, but we do have the promises in His Word to encourage us (Rom. 15:4; Isa. 41:10 and 43:1-5). It was for Paul's sake that God did this, and it was Paul's faith that God honored. What a testimony he was to the people on that storm-tossed ship!

He warned them (vv. 27-32). During the two weeks they had been at sea, the ship had been driven over 500 miles off course and was now adrift in the Adrian Sea. (It is now called the Ionian Sea and must not be confused with the Adriatic Sea.) As the crew took soundings, they discovered that the water was getting more shallow (from 120 feet to 90 feet), indicating that land was near. From the roar of the waves, it appeared that the ship was headed for the rocks.

In order to keep the prow headed toward shore, some of the crew dropped four anchors from the stern. But others of the crew tried to escape from the ship in the dinghy that had been brought on board (v. 16). This was not only an act of selfishness and revolt on their part, but it was also an act of unbelief. Paul had told everybody God's promise that He would keep all those safe who sailed with him on the voyage (v. 24). For the men to abandon ship was to take their lives in their own hands and threaten the lives of others. Whether the soldiers acted wisely in cutting the boat free, it is difficult to determine; but in an emergency, you take emergency measures.

He set a good example before them (vv. 33-38). What a difference it makes when a person has faith in God! Instead of vainly wishing for a change (v. 29) or selfishly trying to escape (v. 30), Paul got ready for the demands that would come at daybreak. It is not difficult to understand why everyone had fasted those two weeks, but now it was time to eat. Caring for one's health is an important part of the Christian life, and even an apostle must not abuse his body.

Paul took the bread and openly prayed and gave thanks to God. (This is a good example for us to follow when we are eating in public places.) His example encouraged the others to join him, and before long, everybody felt better. There are times when one dedicated believer can change the whole atmosphere of a situation simply by trusting God and making that faith visible.

He rescued them (vv. 39-44). When it was day, the pilot saw where they were and made every effort to get the ship to shore. But it was all futile; the ship was grounded and the waves began to beat the stern to pieces. The only thing the passengers could do was jump into the water and make for land.

The soldiers, of course, were concerned about their prisoners; for if a prisoner escaped, the soldier was held accountable and could be killed. Once again, it was Paul whose presence saved their lives. Just as the Lord promised, all of them made it safely to shore, and not one was lost. I have a feeling that Paul had been sharing the Gospel with his fellow passengers and that some of them had trusted in the Lord as a result of this experience. Luke does not give us the details, but would you expect Paul to do otherwise?

Before leaving this exciting section of Acts, we should note some practical lessons that it teaches us. First of all, storms often come when we disobey the will of God. (Jonah is a good example of this truth.) However, it was not Paul who was at fault, but the centurion in charge of the ship. We sometimes suffer because of the unbelief of others.

Second, storms have a way of revealing character. Some of the sailors selfishly tried to escape, others could only hope for the best; but Paul trusted God and obeyed His will.

Third, even the worst storms cannot hide the face of God or hinder the purposes of God. Paul received the word of assurance that they needed, and God overruled so that His servant arrived safely in Rome.

Finally, storms can give us opportunities to serve others and bear witness to Jesus Christ. Paul was the most valuable man on that ship! He knew how to pray, he had faith in God, and he was in touch with the Almighty.

3. Paul the Helper (28:1-10)

God had brought them to the Isle of Malta (which means "refuge"), where the native people welcomed all 276 of them and did their best to make them comfortable. To the Greeks, anybody who did not speak Greek was a "barbarian." These people proved to be kind and sympathetic. The storm abated, but the weather was cold; so the natives built a fire.

After all he had done for the passengers, Paul could well have requested a throne and insisted that everybody serve him! Instead, he did his share of the work and helped gather fuel for the fire. No task is too small for the servant of God who has "the mind of Christ" (Phil. 2:1-13).

One rainy day, a man accompanied by two women arrived at Northfield, hoping to enroll his daughter in D.L. Moody's school for young women. The three needed help in getting their luggage from the railway depot to the hotel, so the visitor "drafted" a rather common-looking man with a horse and wagon, assuming he was a local cabby. The "cabby" said he was waiting for students, but the visitor ordered him to take them to the hotel. The visitor was shocked when the "cabby" did not charge him, and was even more shocked to discover that the "cabby" was D.L. Moody himself! Moody was a leader because he knew how to be a servant.

The episode of the viper reminds us of Paul's experience in Lystra (14:6-18). First, the people thought that Justice, one of their goddesses, had caught up with this notorious prisoner who was supposed to drown in the sea but had somehow escaped. (If only they knew!) When Paul failed to swell up and die, they decided that he must be a god himself! Such are the reasonings of people who judge by appearances.

Was the viper a weapon of Satan to get Paul out of the way? The storm did not drown him, but a hidden trap might catch him. As Christians, we must constantly be alert, for either the serpent or the lion will attack us (2 Cor. 11:3; 1 Peter 5:8). We should also keep in mind that we are being watched, and we must use every opportunity to magnify Christ.

Paul and the party remained on Malta for three months; and, thanks to Paul, they were treated graciously and sent on their way with generous gifts. Since they had lost everything in the shipwreck, the passengers were grateful to have their needs supplied. Luke says nothing about evangelism on the island, but we must believe that Paul shared the Gospel with anybody who would listen. His miraculous deliverance from the sea and from the viper, and his power to heal, would certainly arouse the interest of the people; and Paul would want to give the glory to the Lord (Matt. 5:16).

4. Paul the Preacher (28:11-31)

Whether all 276 people boarded the Alexandrian ship, or just Julius and his guard and prisoners, we do not know; nor do we know why Luke took such care to identify the ship. In Greek mythology, "Castor and Pollux" were the names of the twin sons of Zeus and were revered as the protectors of men on the sea. Many Roman ships bore their image as a plea for safety. It was 80 miles to Syracuse, another 70 to Rhegium, and about 180 to Puteoli, the port of Naples. This time the "south wind" was exactly what they needed in order to make the voyage quickly and safely.

In Puteoli, Paul and his friends, along with Julius and the other prisoners and guards, were urged by the believers to stay and rest for a week; and Julius gave his consent. The centurion knew that Paul had saved their lives, and perhaps he was even getting interested in what these Christians had to offer.

Word had gotten to Rome that Paul was coming; how, we do not know. Perhaps Aristarchus did not go with Paul and Luke on the grain ship, but made his way instead overland to Rome where he met Paul's friends. (At least twenty-six are named in Romans 16.) Or, perhaps a delegation from Caesarea headed for Rome as soon as Paul appealed to Caesar.

Julius and his party took the famous Appian Way and traveled 125 miles from Puteoli to Rome. The first group of Christians met Paul at the Forum of Appius, about forty-three miles from Rome; and the second group met him at the Three Taverns, ten miles nearer to the city. (Some saints will go farther than others!) Paul was greatly encouraged when he met them, as well he might be. Now he could fellowship with the saints and they could be a blessing to one another.

Paul's greatest concern was his witness to the Jews in Rome. They had received no special word about Paul, but they did know that the "Christian sect" was being spoken against in many places (vv. 21-22). When you read Paul's letter to the Romans, you get the impression that the Jews in Rome had misunderstood some of his teachings (Rom. 3:8; 14:1ff). The apostle made it clear that his appeal to Caesar must not be interpreted as an indictment against his nation. Actually, he was a prisoner *on behalf of* his nation and "the hope of Israel."

On the day appointed, Paul spent "from morning till evening" explaining the Scriptures and revealing Christ in the Law and the Prophets. He had "dialogued" this way with the Jews in one synagogue after another, and now he was sharing the Word with the leaders of many synagogues in Rome.

The result? Some were persuaded and some were not. When the Jewish leaders left Paul's house, they were still arguing among themselves! But Paul had faithfully given his witness to the Jews in Rome, and now he would turn to the Gentiles.

Paul quoted the words of Isaiah to these men (Isa. 6:9-10), words that described their tragic spiritual condition. Jesus had used this passage in connection with His parables of the kingdom (Matt. 13:13-15; Mark 4:12; Luke 8:10). The Apostle

John in his Gospel applied them to Israel (12:39-40), and Paul quoted them in his Roman epistle (11:7-8). It is one thing to *listen* and quite something else to *hear*, and there is a great difference between *seeing* and *perceiving*. If anybody should have possessed spiritual understanding, it was these Jewish leaders, but their hearts were dull and hard. Too often those who enjoy the most spiritual privileges are not ready when they must make spiritual decisions.

But their unbelief did not put an end to Paul's ministry of the Gospel! He announced that the Gospel some of the Jews had rejected would be proclaimed to the Gentiles, "and they will hear it!" This is one of the major themes of Acts, how the Gospel moved from the Jews to the Gentiles and from Jerusalem to Rome. Without the Book of Acts, we would turn in the New Testament from the Gospel of John to Romans and ask, "How did the Gospel ever get from the Jews in Jerusalem to the Gentiles in Rome?"

Paul kept "open house" and received anybody who wanted to discuss the things of the kingdom of God. He was chained to a guard who was relieved every six hours, but who was forced to listen as Paul preached and taught and prayed. No wonder some of them were saved! (Phil. 1:12-14; 4:22)

During these two years in Rome, Paul wrote Philippians, Ephesians, Colossians, and Philemon. He expected to be released (Phile. 22; Phil. 1:23-27; 2:24) and most students agree that he was. During this time, he had Timothy with him (Phil. 1:1 and 2:19; Col. 1:1), as well as John Mark, Luke, Aristarchus, Epaphras, Justus, and Demas (Col. 4:10-14; Phile. 24). He also met Philemon's runaway slave Onesimus and led him to faith in Christ (Phile. 10-21). Epaphroditus brought a gift to him from the Philippian church and almost died ministering to Paul (Phil. 2:25-30; 4:18). Tychicus was Paul's "mailman" who delivered Ephesians (Eph. 6:21), Colossians, and Philemon (Col. 4:7-9).

Dr. Luke ended his book before Paul's case had been heard, so he could not give us the results of the trial. We have every reason to believe that Paul was indeed released and that he resumed his ministry, probably traveling as far as Spain (Rom. 15:24, 28). During this period (A.D. 63-66/67), he wrote letters to Timothy and Titus. He left Titus in Crete (Titus 1:5), Trophimus sick in Miletus (2 Tim. 4:20), and Timothy in Ephesus (1 Tim. 1:3). He planned to meet some of his helpers at Nicopolis (Titus 3:12-13) after he had visited some of the churches he had established. Wherever he went, he sought to bring Jews and Gentiles to faith in Jesus Christ.

He was arrested again, probably about the year 67, and this time his situation was changed drastically. He did not live in a house, but was chained in a prison and treated like a criminal (2 Tim. 1:16; 2:9). Winter was coming, and he asked Timothy to bring him his cloak (2 Tim. 4:13). But the saddest thing about this second imprisonment was his being forsaken by the believers in Rome (2 Tim. 4:16-17). The great apostle to the Gentiles was abandoned by the very people he came to assist.

Even Demas forsook him, and only Luke was with him (2 Tim. 4:10-11). The family of Onesiphorus ministered to his needs (2 Tim. 1:16-18), but he longed for Timothy and Mark to come to be at his side (2 Tim. 1:4; 4:9, 21). Paul knew that the end was coming (2 Tim. 4:6-8). Tradition tells us that he was beheaded at Rome in A.D. 67/68.

Luke did not write his book simply to record ancient history. He wrote to encourage the church in every age to be faithful to the Lord and carry the Gospel to the ends of the earth. "What was begun with so much heroism ought to be continued with ardent zeal," said Charles Spurgeon, "since we are assured that the same Lord is mighty still to carry on His heavenly designs."

"Lo, I am with you always!"

Therefore, *be daring!*

Dear Reader:

We would like to know your opinion of **Be Daring.** Your ideas will help us as we strive to continue offering books that will satisfy your needs and interests.

Send your responses to: **VICTOR BOOKS**
1825 College Avenue
Wheaton, IL 60187

What most influenced your decision to purchase this book?
- ☐ Front Cover
- ☐ Title
- ☐ Author
- ☐ Back cover material

- ☐ Price
- ☐ Length
- ☐ Subject
- ☐ Other: _____

What did you like about this book?
- ☐ Helped me understand myself better
- ☐ Helped me understand others better
- ☐ Helped me understand the Bible

- ☐ Helped me understand God
- ☐ It was easy to teach
- ☐ Author
- ☐ Good reference tool

How was this book used?
- ☐ For my personal reading
- ☐ Studied it in a group situation
- ☐ Used it to teach a group

- ☐ As a reference tool
- ☐ For a church or school library

If you used this book to teach a group, did you also use the accompanying leader's guide?   ☐ YES ☐ NO

Please indicate your level of interest in reading other Victor Books like this one.
- ☐ Very interested
- ☐ Somewhat interested

- ☐ Not very interested
- ☐ Not at all interested

Would you recommend this book to a friend? ☐ YES   ☐ NO

Please indicate your age.
   ☐ Under 18   ☐ 25-34   ☐ 45-54
   ☐ 18-24   ☐ 35-44   ☐ 55 or over

Would you like to   NAME: _____
receive more infor-
mation about Victor   ADDRESS: _____
Books? If so,
please fill in your   _____
name and address.

Do you have additional comments or suggestions regarding Victor Books?